L I F E

MEDITATIONS

L I F E

MEDITATIONS

Thoughts and Quotations for All of Life's Moments

BY EDWARD J. LAVIN, S.J.

WINGS BOOKS•NEW YORK•AVENEL, NEW JERSEY

This 1993 edition is published by Wings Books,
distributed by Outlet Book Company, Inc.,
a Random House Company,
40 Engelhard Avenue, Avenel, New Jersey 07001.

Random House
New York · Toronto · London · Sydney · Auckland

Design: Nora Sheehan

Jacket art: Waterlilies (detail), Claude Monet

Printed and bound in the United States of America

Library of Congress Cataloging-in-Publication Data
Lavin, Edward J.
    Life meditations / by Edward J. Lavin.
        p.   cm.
    Includes bibliographical references.
    ISBN 0-517-09374-X
    1. Spiritual life—Meditations.   I. Title.
BL624.2.L385   1993
291.4'3—dc20   93-25024
                                    CIP

8 7 6 5 4 3 2

ABOUT THE AUTHOR

Father Edward J. Lavin is a Jesuit priest and an artist who has taught theology, art and Zen meditation. This book combines his love of all things beautiful and thoughts spiritual.

I dedicate this book to God.

INTRODUCTION

IN THIS SERIES of reflections the image of the journey is used frequently. I use it not only because it is a fuel for the imagination and a powerful source of motivation for the emotions and ideas that give energy to our lives but also because it is flexible and allows for other important images.

For example, the journey allows us to imagine that there are stages in the voyage, various degrees of perfection and completion. If I read this book and think that I should have already achieved all the little perfections that are held up as ideals, I might easily become discouraged and anxious. We must realize that these are increasing stages in the ideals we have set up here.

The image of the journey is also useful in that it suggests a need to deal with external realities. There are roadblocks and detours in all of our lives, and I would like, in this book, to deal with some of them. But not only with the negatives; I have tried to touch upon many of the wonderful downhill slopes, too, as well as the surprises of beautiful landscapes. In short, this book is a map, nothing but that. Each of us is our own guide in our travels.

We human beings have the unique opportunity of the inward journey—that search for our own growth and the perfection of our minds and imaginations and emotions. This trip is also filled with obstacles and some dangers—dark deceptions and obstinate, foolish forms of ego. Perhaps one or more of these reflections will put a light in your hands, some small illumination of the path.

The paintings are also meant to be illuminations. Landscapes of the heart and mind. Maps of mystery. Use them with pleasure.

Perhaps this book will lead you to some of the joys and satisfactions of a well-ordered mind, a pregnant imagination, and an emotional life tamed to your purposes. But easy does it! Not even the most exalted saint; not even Saint Francis of Assisi nor the Buddha could look on these reflections with perfect aplomb.

Remember, they are indications of stages in a journey of self-examination, a journey that I hope you will undertake. Perhaps there are paragraphs that will help you at certain moments in your life. Others might not pertain to where you are today, but you might find them interesting and return to them at another time in your journey.

I hope that these *Life Meditations* will help you to move forward on a daily basis with strength, serenity and joy.

EDWARD J. LAVIN, S.J.

YOUR OUTER LIFE

Achievement
Action
Attention
Attitude
Balance
Burdens
Change
Creativity
Crisis
Evil
Failure
Family
Friendship
Goals
Growth
Health
Helping Others
Humor
Interests
Pain
Perfection
Play
Relationships
Security
Service
Sharing
Success
Work

ACHIEVEMENT

"To strive, to seek, to find, and not to yield."
—ALFRED, LORD TENNYSON

THE ROMAN POET Horace held up his life's work to us and said with fierce pride, "I have raised a monument more lasting than bronze." He was satisfied with the achievement of his life.

All of us are held to achieve something with our lives. We are given a ball of clay that is ourselves and the small portion of the world that most nearly touches us. We are called to form something out of that clay.

A self that habitually loves—that is a form. A life that touches and nurtures others—that is a form. A work that is creative and full of thought and beauty—that is a form. How glorious is the person who has achieved all this! How sad the existence of the person who has done nothing.

In a rare spark of wisdom *The New York Times* crossword puzzle sets us the following bon mot to solve: "Youth is a gift of nature, but old age is a work of art."

Do we see ourselves and our achievements as a work of art?

I am elated when I stand in the strong presence of the person who has achieved, who has erected a monument to life.

On the contrary, I am frightened by the stagnant weakness of the person who has allowed the virus of inaction to infect his life.

We can achieve a life and a work.

Be an achiever! Make yourself a proud, happy person.

THE LOWER GORGE OF THE GRAND CANYON, ARIZONA, THOMAS MORAN

ACHIEVEMENT

"Man's nature, his passions and anxieties, are a cultural product; as a matter of fact, man himself is the most important creation and achievement of the continuous human effort, the record of what we call history."

—ERICH FROMM

DID YOU EVER see a young child win a prize? His little face is suffused with joy. His small body trembles with excitement; his eyes shine with pride. This lovely display of open happiness moves us very much. It displays an openness of emotion that we adults sometimes try to hide. Of course we can try to suppress our emotions, but like so many other things, the child's responses also exist in the adult, only more or less clearly. To be childlike is an achievement.

Naturally we don't always get prizes for our achievements, nor do these achievements have to be written in heroic verse. Thank God that our lives are not all *Illiad*s or *Odyssey*s. How tiring that would be.

Many of our actions may seem like small achievements—such as the fact that our children have been well cared for today—or they may be more extensive—a life well lived, a relationship well nourished, a work beautifully finished. But whether they seem large or small, we should allow ourselves the excitement and pride of the sense of achievement. How wonderful to feel so good about ourselves!

WHEATFIELD AND CYPRESS TREES, VINCENT VAN GOGH

ACTION

IN ALL RELIGIONS there is a certain tension between "contemplatives" and "activists." The contemplatives remain cloistered and pray and make saints of themselves. The activists help others in both a spiritual and a physical sense. Buddhists tend to be more contemplative, while Hindus are more activist. American churches have often been accused of excessive activism.

As with so many other dualities, the truth tends to be in the middle—a bit of contemplation and a bit of activism. The great Jesuit anthropologist-mystic Teilhard de Chardin put it simply: Our lives should be actively creative, with periods of peace to refresh the soul.

All this may seem a bit esoteric to a person leading a "normal" life. But even we more common folk must keep our eyes on the stars and try to lead lives of more uncommon intensity. We have to be active, but active about things that sometimes transcend the humdrum. In the midst of this activity we also need our times of quiet to fill our souls with the rhythm of God.

SUMMER AT THE HAMPTONS, DENISE ABADY

ATTENTION

"On some preference esteem is based; to esteem everything is to esteem nothing."
—MOLIÈRE

How SPLENDID IT is to be able to pay attention. The movements of the mind are various. We can use it to sweep across reality like a great spotlight, illuminating vast acres of facts and feelings, or we can stop the sweep and focus in on a specific facet of reality.

Attention is a splendid thing. Teachers wait for the exhilarating moment when the mind of a student zooms in on a subject. This kind of growth in the human mind is beautiful.

There are many people who don't seem to be able to do this—to pay attention. How superficial their perception must be. Butterflies are beautiful but flighty.

Attention can be trained. But first we must be convinced of its necessity and importance. How important is it anyway to be able to understand something fully? Not at all, if we don't mind being identified as superficial. But I don't know anyone who glories in that.

The most beautiful moments in ballet come when the dancer is concentrating on her whole body, even to the tips of her fingers. Makarova was a master at this. That's why she moved us so much.

Let's pay attention to ourselves and to those around us. Let's pay attention to life. Look. Listen. Focus. Experience. Enjoy. Be there for the ride!

THE GREAT ODALISQUE, JEAN AUGUSTE DOMINIQUE INGRES

ATTITUDE

"I finally figured out that the only reason to be alive is to enjoy it."
—RITA MAE BROWN

THE ANCIENTS THOUGHT THAT there were four "humors" (personality traits) in humans. These were the temperaments: phlegmatic, sanguine, melancholy, and choleric. Perhaps we could update these a little by renaming them laidback, hopeful, sad, and angry, respectively. Each one of us has all four of the humors, but usually only one predominates. We might ask ourselves: Am I mostly laid back? Optimistic? Depressed? Angry? Of course there are a whole battery of modern attitudes. How do I see myself and how do others see me? Am I anxious, fearful, negative, positive, violent, aggressive, active, passive? Do I see myself as having a superattitude: a spotlight in my psyche that shines outward and illuminates my world? Are all who come into contact with me made red by the light of my choleric disposition? Or do my passivity and negativity dull my life down to grey?

Surely they do! Have the courage and patience to find your color—and choose it. Why not be like the saint whose goodness shines on the world around him as a golden halo. Let gold be your color.

WATERLILIES: THE MORNING *(left detail)*, CLAUDE MONET

ATTITUDE

"I am the Greatest!"

—Muhammad Ali

THE WORD ATTITUDE has taken on a new, more restrictive meaning, usually with the connotation of "bad attitude" as in "I sense in you an attitude" or "The meeting was charged with an attitude."

Expanding the word into its older, more useful meaning of a general show of one's disposition, I think that we can explore the concept of attitude in a fruitful way. Attitude is the first face we show to the outside world. It can be physical, as in "body language." If my whole body is leaning toward the door, it shows clearly how much I want out of a boring or upsetting circumstance. Again, in some mysterious way our inner attitude radiates a meaning easily read.

Our attitudes betray our most secret thoughts and emotions. No matter how we try to hide them, they leak out somehow and display us with all the gross openness of an anatomical chart. Sometimes if we look at them carefully enough, they can reveal things about us that we ourselves were not aware of. We can make our attitudes an important tool of self-knowledge. It's a face we may or may not like, but it's one that's always with us. And yes, when we know our attitudes, we can change them.

LADY WITH HAT AND FEATHER BOA, GUSTAV KLIMT

BALANCE

"To see a world in a grain of sand
and a heaven in a wild flower;
Hold infinity in the palm of your hand,
And eternity in an hour."
—WILLIAM BLAKE, *Auguries of Innocence*

IT IS AN ASTOUNDING sight to see the thousands and thousands of Chinese people gather in parks every morning to practice t'ai chi. These gentle exercises performed en masse are like some great spiritual river—a flow of such immense proportions that it takes the breath away.

All of these many minds and bodies are intent on improving the balance of the life force within them. They are each dedicated to making and keeping themselves *whole*. The entire experience comprises a force of nature.

We in the West don't think much in terms of balance, and obviously we should. Even the very thought of an exquisite union and balance of all of our forces, both physical and mental, has a gentle, hopeful ring to it.

Not all of us are going to practice t'ai chi, but all of us must find a bridge between our physical and spiritual parts. When that balance is achieved, what a happy comfort for ourselves!

Mimoses, Anemones, and Leaves in a Blue Vase, Odilon Redon

BALANCE

"The best and safest thing is to keep a balance in your life, acknowledge the great powers around us and in us. If you can do that, and live that way, you are really a wise man."
—EURIPIDES

SOMETIMES IT CAN be helpful to use the pendulum as an image to show the delicate balance between truth and happiness. Swing too far to the side of "truth" and the pendulum indicates a position that is too rigid and exclusive, that ignores all the textures of real life. If the pendulum swings too far to that of "happiness," we enter into an area in which there are no perceptible absolutes—a place of flaws and instability. "This is true because I want it to be true." There is no concern for history or experience, just an explosive mixture of something that seems "true" because I "feel" it to be so.

When the pendulum is at its low point—the point of greatest power and velocity —we can arrive at the sweet truth, a balance of general principals and experience.

There are other balances that are basic to our well-being. The delicate balance of our emotions—anxiety tempered by hope, for example. The interplay of emotions and thought, body and soul, interior and exterior. The good lies somewhere in the middle.

WATERLILY POND, HARMONY GREEN, CLAUDE MONET

BURDENS

"So we beat on, boats against the current, borne back ceaselessly into the past."
—F. Scott Fitzgerald, *The Great Gatsby*

Fire island is an odd place off the coast of Long Island, New York. One of its oddest characteristics is that there are no roads on the island, just narrow wooden boardwalks. So there are no cars on this little place, only bicycles and little red wagons in which everything is carried: groceries and baggage and babies and two-by-fours. Imagine, lines of people pulling their little red wagons. Charming, picturesque, deliberately simple.

Let us cut from this symbolically simple scene to a larger, more profound image. Imagine, if you will, the same little red wagons being pulled around against the setting of a great city. Each person pulls his wagon behind him wherever he goes. The wagons bump into one another, topple over curbs, and create a general disorder. They are not carrying the small necessities of life but the burdens of our pasts, each of us dragging around his past wherever he goes.

So there we are, attached to the vicious memories of our past. Why did I say that to my boss? A hurtful memory—right back in the wagon. Why did I do that to my wife? A shameful, guilt-ridden memory. Back into the little red wagon. And so we go through life, attached to and victimized by the past.

Do you think that this obsession with the past affects our ability to live happily in the present? Of course it does. We have to get rid of those little red carriers of hurt. Let go of those wagons!

On the Beach, Edouard Manet

CHANGE

"You could not step twice into the same river; for other waters are ever flowing on to you."
—HERACLITUS, *On the Universe*

HERACLITUS WAS A Greek philosopher who thought that the whole metaphysics of reality could be explained by the idea of change. Visualize this favorite saying of his that tells us you can never put your foot into a river twice at the same point. The notion that our lives are in a constant state of flux is an unsettling one, more so when we recognize that there are certain constants in our lives that seem essential—rocks and roots that give us rest from free flow.

Like all truths, however, there is another side that is equally important. In our search for stability we can seek a life in which there is no change. We become like a mollusk attached to the side of a rock, indifferent to the tides of change and the waves of new situations. A person who never changes escapes from risks, but he also misses all the energy and excitement of new life. The river passes him by unnoticed. Stability is necessary to all of us, but the constant newness of the flow of life gives us an excitement and a beauty that are also absolutely necessary. Go with the flow.

MAGICAL MOMENT OF CHANGE, SUSANNE NYBERG

CREATIVITY

*"Someday perhaps the inner light will shine forth from us,
and then we shall need no other light."*

—Johann Wolfgang von Goëthe

THE JESUIT THEOLOGIAN Teilhard de Chardin sees our entire world, indeed the entire universe, as a great evolutionary movement toward perfection. He sees us all creating a universe that is more and more related in unity. This vast dream is thrilling, but it leaves each one of us with an intense responsibility. We are each of us called to make the world a better place. Our lives must be creative. We are not talking here about making potholders; we are talking about the difficult human activity that produces a new, serious object or relationship or idea.

Just as our spiritual life is lost unless we help others, so is our emotional and psychological life a barren thing unless it is put to serious, positive purpose. The great art of Michelangelo is reflected in all the positive actions of our life. Creativity puts order into chaos, life into the inert, and beauty into the ordinary. In this scheme examples of creativity could include sweeping the street or balancing the books. The question for each of us is, Do our actions somehow make the world better?

SUNSET, ODILON REDON

CREATIVITY

"A work of art is a corner of creation seen through a temperament."
—EMILE ZOLA

THERE IS A FOUNTAIN of creativity in each of us. But in many of us there are muds of indolence and stones of fear that block the flow of this clear water. How essential is creative activity to our lives and happiness?

There are many ways in which we contact outside reality. Our senses supply us with raw sensuous data—colors and feels and tastes and odors—rich cognitive material. Our minds set forth what we receive into neat, orderly conceptual rows. What more do we need? Why do we have to rearrange things, put our own stamp on the infinitely curious clay of the world?

To put it simplistically, we are creative because the opportunity is there. We create because we have to. Mozart had no choice. On a less intense level we create because as we change reality, we change ourselves into someone more energetic and more powerful.

When we hurl our fiery ax into the untended woods of the world, we create something new, like a god touching the lifeless finger of matter. Creativity makes us someone, and we deserve this power.

YOUNG GIRLS AT PIANO, PIERRE-AUGUSTE RENOIR

CRISIS

"The storm had rolled away to faintness like a wagon crossing a bridge."
—EUDORA WELTY

IN SPITE OF the terrible aspects of our lives we can, in a lighthearted way, compare them to a gameboard. At the throw of the dice we move ahead seven spaces and land in the cave of the fiery dragon, or on Broadway with two hotels on it. Another throw of the dice and we jump into the space of the grisly Black Knight. What awful luck!

Our lives are like this all the way from our first day of school, through adolescence, marriage, and old age—and finally to death, the ultimate bad luck.

As chaotic as all this might be, we have to learn to handle it. First we have to realize that we can do something about all these ups and downs of life. It's not some great cosmic toss of the dice. And then the plan might go like this:

"Accept the things I cannot change.
Have the courage to change the things I can,
And the wisdom to know the difference."

HIGH CLIFF, COAST OF MAINE, WINSLOW HOMER

CRISIS

"Great emergencies and crises show us how much greater our vital resources are than we had supposed."

—William James

THERE ARE POINTS in our lives when everything reaches a critical mass and we are ready to explode. These crises are almost always thought of as terrifying moments. But in fact these crucial turning points can be used as important times of learning. Usually a crisis is brought on by excess, by ourselves, or by what seem to be unmanageable circumstances. If we spot it in time, we can reduce the critical mass and look at what brought it on. We can search for the cause as we try to calm the tremors brought on by this situation. Where is the excess? Was I pushing myself too hard? Was I bending my nature in some unnatural way? Why did circumstances and people add too much heat to my existence?

There are answers to these questions. Lucky are those who discover them. Those who don't find the answers are condemned to the misadventures of other crises, each one more explosive than the other. We must not confront the dangers of life without adequate understanding. Simplicity has its own rewards but not always!

Rocks at l'Estaque, Paul Cezanne

EVIL

"What doesn't destroy me, makes me stronger."
—FRIEDERICH NIETZSCHE

THE FOUR HORSEMEN—Famine, Disease, War, and Death—come roaring down out of the black clouds. The thunder of their hooves makes our hearts tremble and freezes our minds.

Many philosophers have pondered this problem. Saint Thomas Aquinas tells us that evil is merely the absence of good. Tell that to the Holocaust survivors. The Buddha says that we can't suffer if we don't desire anything. Tell that to the mother of the child who has just been diagnosed with cancer.

It is a vicious problem, and no one really has an answer. Some people do, however, have a method of coping.

Large principles have a way of easing the pain of small afflictions. It is in the small crevices of life that we find the small evils—meanness, jealousy, enmity, and so forth. All these small evils can be handled by the larger principles of detachment or love or resignation. The small is covered by the large.

But the large evils—the Holocaust, the fatal diseases, the Bangladesh floods, the Somali famines, and so on—all of these need the moral principles—justice, charity, the great love, and God, the greatest Love of all.

And so, I confront the four horsemen with the light and sharpness of moral weapons. Justice is my sword, trust is my dagger, and God is my shield.

Town, Alexandra A. Exter

FAILURE

"Nothing to look backward to with pride,
And nothing to look forward to with hope."
—ROBERT FROST, "The Death of the Hired Man"

THE ONLY REAL failures I know are people whose lives are consumed with greed or egotism or meanness or despair. These are my norms of judgment, and I know that they differ from the acceptable norms of our society. I know also that I am deliberately exposing the dark sides of the perfectly legitimate goals of material possessions and self-interest.

I present this paradox to illustrate dramatically how different our perceptions of the norms of success and failure might be. I myself prefer the deeper goals of happiness and depth of soul and mind—wisdom.

The notion of failure is so subjective: the nonattainment of self-imposed goals, an arrow short or wide of the target, a journey to a disappointing destination, a light on a barren landscape. These are our failures, not those imposed on us by a silly or superficial culture.

I don't want to imply that there are no objective norms. A person who does not live up to his or her obligations—a husband who does not assure the security of his family, for instance—is a gross failure. But I urge self-constructed norms. We deserve this kind of freedom.

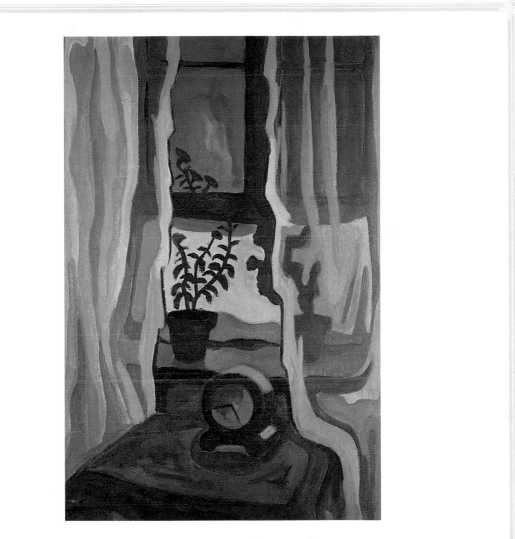

The Open Window, Karl Schmidt-Rottluff

FAMILY

"The family is one of nature's masterpieces."

—GEORGE SANTAYANA

WE ARE CHARMED when we see a family of animals on the nature programs on TV. The young are so innocent in their play. A group of young cheetahs jumping on each other's tails makes us all happy. We are moved by the ferocity and courage of the mother as she provides for her young and defends them against their enemies. And we are instinctively drawn when nature arranges that the father animal takes part in this drama. The family calls to us over the ages and across the differences of species.

The idea and the feeling of the family are so essential and so deeply rooted in us that oddly enough we can sometimes forget about its importance. But when the dissolution of the family begins to threaten our culture, then we feel a terror of nature that is primal.

I think that we are awash in the meltdown of the essentials of our entire culture.

We ache and yearn for the stability of the family, so why not turn our concern to the family instead of to ourselves? Not "me" but "we"! Not the body politic but the loving circle of the family. Not the speculative idea but the real warmth and giving of the family.

STILL LIFE WITH FLOWERS—INTERIOR OF THE ARTIST'S APARTMENT,
PAUL GAUGUIN

FRIENDSHIP

"What is a friend? A single soul dwelling in two bodies."

—ARISTOTLE

LET US TAKE an example. Once I was very sick. It was clear that the cure for this illness was in my own hands. However, it involved two things that I found most difficult to do—exercise and good diet. Most of the people I knew, aware of my detestation for broccoli and walking, never mentioned these hateful things. Two of my closest friends, however, were really pests. "Good food, good food, walk, walk, walk." I would have liked to have killed them. But, and this is the point, which of these were my real friends—those who were so nice that they never mentioned the hateful remedies or those who so loved my life that they made me miserable until I changed my ways?

There is something basic about friendship. It is like the structure that holds up a building. Not beautiful in itself, it supports the beauty. It is mostly hidden and absolutely essential.

Friendships are mostly taken for granted, and yet, as the poet Gerard Manley Hopkins says about the Virgin Mary, they may be compared to "the air we breathe," so important are they.

Friendship is not dramatic, so it is hardly noticed until it is needed. It may sound odd but friendship is more substantial and rarer than love. We are blessed by our friends.

Two Boys Rowing, Winslow Homer

FRIENDSHIP

"The most I can do for my friend is simply to be his friend."
—HENRY DAVID THOREAU

IT IS A PECULIAR and almost banal observation that we can be separated from a friend for a long time and pick up where we left off. This is not always true of a lover—a relationship that seems to be more delicate and needs more nurturing. Why is this? Does the close intimacy needed for love preclude the sturdy surety of friendship? Maybe so. But more certainly the needs and expectancies of lovers are different from those of friends. My friend will give me what I need, especially his presence and support. I don't ask from him, nor do I need the semiobsessional gifts that I might ask from a lover.

There are miraculous things about friendship. I have a good friend who lives in a foreign country and I see him rarely. When we do meet, he always says to me, "Don't get too tired." This simple statement is so charged with past experience— good times and bad, happiness and suffering—that it can force me to reexamine my entire life—my health and my emotional and spiritual stability. "Don't get too tired." It is said with such affection and concern that I am more deeply moved by it than by almost anything else in my life.

My friends are the support of my life.

Path in Papeete, Paul Gauguin

GOALS

"Climb high
Climb far
Your goal the sky
Your aim the star."

—Anonymous

I KNOW A PRIEST who has an enormous tractor trailer. His vacation each year is to set out in this monster and drive around the West and Midwest. This is only strange because he never plans his trips—he just gets in and goes. It's a sort of existential journey, a twelve-wheeled Tao careening around the Rocky Mountains. He is an artist and is used to the risks of the unknown. Most people would find great anxiety in this kind of journey without a destination.

And yet many people travel through life without any conscious goals. They get up each morning, eat breakfast, go to work, come home, eat dinner, watch TV, and go to bed, make love perhaps, conceive a baby perhaps, and go to sleep. This is called a normal life—yet the routine without meaning is the empty life. It's as if their routine was self-explanatory, and of course it is not. How meaningful is a life without goals?

The life that is unexamined and unfocused is dreary beyond limit—a gray, plodding schedule of repetition. How much more exciting to be able to say, "I am living my life to express my love," or "I do all this for my family," or "I do this to create myself," or, most thrilling of all, "The goal of my life is to get closer to God." If I shoot an arrow into the air, who cares? When I transfix my target, we all care—a lot.

Mont St. Victoire, Paul Cezanne

GROWTH

*"Either you reach a higher point today, or you exercise your strength
in order to be able to climb higher tomorrow."*
—FRIEDRICH NIETZSCHE

THERE ARE CERTAIN myths and old stories about growth that are very powerful, if unconscious, motives of feeling. The mustard seed that grows into a gigantic tree; the Tree of Knowledge; the fearsome power of the giants—all these stories move us to deep levels of meaning and feeling.

We are all constrained by the natural rhythms of growth. We love little things; children and puppies charm us. Part of that charm is the fact that there are new beginnings, a memory of what we once were. But nature is inexorable—even children and puppies must grow up. Their bodies will mature, nature will take care of that. But what of the children's emotions and minds? We, not nature, must take care of that.

There is nothing charming about a sixty-year-old man who acts like a teenager. Equally disconcerting is the grandmother who plays the role of the subdeb. These kinds of people are not normal—happily so—but in most of us are some limits of growth. We don't want that; we want to allow ourselves the freedom to grow into whatever we are capable of or desire to be. We must somehow feel the force and the strength of the great oak in ourselves. There is no stopping us. We should become the great works of art of our whole lives.

Among the Sierra Nevada Mountains, California, Albert Bierstadt

GROWTH

*"We must not stay as we are, doing always what was done last time,
or we shall stick in the mud."*

—George Bernard Shaw

THERE ARE ABOUT one million people who think that they can create master-pieces like Jackson Pollock's just by dripping paint. They never succeed because Pollock, from long practice, has the line of the growth of nature instinctive in his hand. There is a line of growth in nature, and all natural things have it. Think of the branch of a tree. Sometimes it shoots out free and unencumbered; sometimes it must twist upward to find the sun; sometimes it must reinforce itself to bear the weight of other branches and leaves. But grow it does, easily or tortuously—and when it stops growing, it dies.

And thus our own growth—sometimes easy, sometimes tortuous. Our own suns and weights determine our direction of growth. The physical and the psychological —lights and burdens. We let ourselves be shaped like branches and we continue to grow like nature, into a beautiful thing.

THE GARDEN AT GIVERNY, CLAUDE MONET

HEALTH

"Health is the first muse, comprising the magical benefits of air, landscape, and exercise on the mind."

—Ralph Waldo Emerson

THE IMAGE THAT medical science gives us of health is that of a body free of all the alien entities that can attack the cells and interfere with their proper functioning. A healthy system then, is one free of pollution and enemy forms. This is a good definition.

But beyond this, well beyond, is another, more integral idea of health. It is predicated on a belief that the life force in each of us must be able to flow freely. There is no separation of mind and body; we are a dynamic unity, a path of energy. This way incorporates the whole person—the food, the gentle exercise, the state of mind—all of these components together keep us healthy.

We need to keep the whole from flying off kilter so that all the parts remain strong and energetic. Holistic medicine is not named that for nothing.

We have to work on our health. It is one of the most important things in our lives.

APPLES AND ORANGES, PAUL CEZANNE

HEALTH

"We must first be a good animal."
—Ralph Waldo Emerson

UNTIL RECENTLY it has been a well-kept secret that good health deeply affects the direction and purpose of our lives. When we feel good, we do more, we think better, we have more fun. When our bodies are tuned, our minds are clear, and then we move in the right direction.

The young are generally gifted with good health. They take it for granted and coast for years. But sports bring the body into focus. Athletes take meticulous care of their bodies. They know best about fine-tuning. Most of us are careless about this precious gift. We don't exercise or eat properly. We abuse this most precious and complex mechanism.

We don't miss our good health until it betrays us. Or have we betrayed ourselves? We can't imagine the catastrophic effect that a serious illness such as cancer can cause. It weakens the body, clouds the mind, and darkens the spirit. It's a long, hard road to recovery. For the fortunate.

Let's first be good animals. It feels good to take care of ourselves. It's our physical, mental, and spiritual health that prayer and meditation, exercise and proper eating, can strengthen. So much is in our hands.

CLIFFS OF THE UPPER COLORADO RIVER, WYOMING TERRITORY,
THOMAS MORAN

HELPING OTHERS

"Give me your tired, your poor,
Your huddled masses yearning to breathe free,
The wretched refuse of your teeming shore,
Send these, the homeless, tempest tossed to me,
I lift my lamp beside the golden door!"
—EMMA LAZARUS, *Inscription for the Statue of Liberty*

SPIRITUAL TEACHINGS say that unless the powers we develop in ourselves are directed outward for the benefit of others, they will atrophy and dry up within us. A circuit has to be completed—from our souls to others and back to ourselves.

Besides, unless our hearts are open, we can easily become indifferent to the brutality of the world. Imagine being indifferent to the suffering of a starving child, or a homeless woman, or the spiritual desolation of a friend.

This indifference to the world is felt more often than we would like to think. Many people cultivate their own little secret gardens and never open the gates to others. But we must realize that the other is absolutely essential to our spiritual health. The virus of self-absorption is deadly and has only one cure—compassion.

It looks great stuffed in any stocking

Give SOAP OPERA DIGEST and save 38%!

☐ **Yes!** I know a great gift idea when I see one. Send a SOAP OPERA DIGEST holiday gift subscription to the person I've named below. Also, send me a special holiday gift card so I can announce my gift.* I'll pay just $39.95 for 26 fabulous issues. I save 38% off the cover price.

SEND A SOAP OPERA DIGEST HOLIDAY GIFT SUBSCRIPTION TO:

Name _____
Please Print

Address _____ Apt. _____

City _____ State _____ Zip _____

FROM:

My name is _____
Please Print

My address is _____ Apt. _____

City _____ State _____ Zip _____

☐ Payment enclosed

☐ Bill me after the holidays   **For faster service call 1-800-544-7846**

Please allow 6-8 weeks for delivery of first issue. Annual newsstand price is $64.74. Published biweekly. Foreign orders must add $10 per year for postage and be prepaid in U.S. currency. Gift orders will begin with the new year if received by December 1.

*For orders received after Dec. 1, gift card will be sent directly to recipient.

2ALD5

BUSINESS REPLY MAIL

FIRST CLASS MAIL   PERMIT NO. 1102   BOULDER, CO

Postage will be paid by:

PO BOX 55124
BOULDER, CO 80323-5124

BLUE WATERLILIES, CLAUDE MONET

HELPING OTHERS

"You're either part of the solution or part of the problem."

—ELDRIDGE CLEAVER

THERE ARE SOME stark choices presented us by modern philosophy. If they remained in the unearthly levels of philosophy, there wouldn't be much harm done. But these high concepts tend to leak down into popular culture. And we are faced with some "immutable" truths, such as the concept of unlimited freedom or the nonstructure of relativism. The most pernicious of these absolutes is Jean-Paul Sartre's famous statement "Hell is the other person."

Is this abhorrent idea a given in our modern culture? I suppose that selfishness has always been with us, but is the cult of self more evident in contemporary culture? It seems that it might be—there are so many devotees of self among us.

And yet history and the traditional philosophy and even some psychology—in short, the wisdom of the ages—teach us the contrary, that at least one important source of happiness for us flows from our concern for others.

Of course, our own experience is our ultimate judge of the truth. Do we feel better as a result of helping others? The power of that feeling can develop direction and urgency in our lives. Tenderness and compassion bring their own warmth to us, and hell is really not helping the other person.

FLOWERS IN A COPPER POT, VINCENT VAN GOGH

HUMOR

WE DO NOT UNDERSTAND about humor. And although I hesitate to say that animals don't tell jokes, I am inclined to think that joke telling is a strictly human quality. A good laugh is fun, but what is it for? I think I know some answers.

Humor is a proper response to life's little (and big) absurdities. Those slides of nonreason need the cushions of laughter.

Humor allows us not to fall victim to the sorrows and tragedies of our existence. Wallowing in pangs of being a victim leads nowhere. Laugh it off, my friend.

The completely humorless person is a disaster. Sepulchral in his rusty chains and tattletale gray sheets, he is a black hole in the fabric of civilized life. Who can abide him? Who wants to be near him? Who wants even to know him? A person who complains all the time is a humorless person, as is the person who always emphasizes the negative poles of life.

But we who have humor, like Don Quixote, face the windmills and dragons of absurdity. Laughter is our lance and wit our shield. We defy you, Life, and we enjoy ourselves doing it.

Mona Lisa, Leonardo da Vinci

HUMOR

"Life is a jest; and all things show it;
I thought so once, but now I know it."

—JOHN GAY, *"My Own Epitaph"*

WHAT A DRAB, BARREN DESERT is a life without humor. Without it we can become overwhelmed by all the little and big sadnesses and trials and tragedies.

An actress I know who was consumed by depression decided to look in the mirror to see how her face appeared in that state. When she saw herself, she broke into laughter at the absurdity of the situation—her depression used professionally.

Life is absurd—a funhouse of conflicting demands, unimagined events, and clownish persons. We can confront this maelstrom with despair, as Sartre did, or with humor, as Chaplin did.

Laughter is a great healing gift, and the people who cause laughter are worldly saints. A favorite image for Christ in art is the clown—the holy clown.

There are people with no sense of humor. The follies of life can crush them. But the person with humor can fly above the heavy weights of life. A cascade of laughter is a miraculous bath—a cleansing of the spirit.

ROSES UNDER THE TREES, GUSTAV KLIMT

INTERESTS

"One ought, every day at least, to hear a little song, read a good poem, see a fine picture, and, if it were possible, to speak a few reasonable words."

—JOHANN WOLFGANG VON GOETHE

PLAIN OATMEAL IS not interesting, nor is a lot of the work we do, nor much of the conversation we have. Our interests should be interesting. A child who sits and bounces a ball all day in the same place might be a cause for some concern. The child who is learning to juggle has caught onto the joy of life and is very interesting.

A person without many interests is not doomed, but he is living a life without spice—a mess of plain porridge, wholesome but dull.

There are so many splendid sparks of life to enthrall us. Art, literature, dance, the theater, travel, hobbies, creative activities, and more, can transport us to different, more consuming realms of living. Spice—hot pepper to our pizza—an open, roaring, electric life.

There are so many interests for a person who is interested—great gifts ready to be opened and enjoyed. Dry and dull is not doom, but who wants it? We would rather fly on the wings of stimulation and interest.

VASE WITH RED POPPIES, ODILON REDON

PAIN

"Grace strikes us when we are in great pain and restlessness . . .
Sometimes at that moment a wave of light breaks into our darkness,
and it is as though a voice were saying: 'You are accepted.' "
—PAUL TILLICH

ALL THE MYTHOLOGIES tell us that at the beginning there was a time of great happiness—in Atlantis, for example, or the Garden of Eden. Then something happened, and pain and suffering entered into the world. The human condition implies pain.

This painful situation has been faced in various ways. The Stoics thought that we should ignore pain. Modern medical science seeks to eradicate it. But many Stoics ended by slitting their wrists in baths of warm water. Moreover, tuberculosis had all but disappeared, yet here it is again eating its way through lungs in an epidemic fashion.

I don't think we can ignore pain, nor do I think that all the splendors of modern medicine can end it completely.

I do think that as part of the human condition pain will be insistently with us. I think each of us has to learn to live with it and to find our own way of dealing with it. This will have something to do, I am sure, with our mental attitude. A positive mental attitude is a certain remedy for pain.

HEAD OF CHRIST, KARL SCHMIDT-ROTTLUFF

PAIN

"Fire is the test of gold; adversity, of strong men."

—SENECA

PAIN IS ONE OF the most universal experiences that are almost impossible to describe. Pain lives in us, parallel to our lives; it gnaws at our senses; it tears apart our consciousness; it is the monstrous enemy. We have all experienced it, and the most important question is how do we handle it.

I saw a woman once who by meditation, by making quiet her mind, was able to change the raging fire of her pain to a gentle reminder of her mortality. The mind can have enormous influence on physical pain, and it is the very arena of psychic pain that is in some ways worse than physical pain. The fire in the mind can be controlled by moral and spiritual balance.

So it now seems that the mind is an important analgesic in blunting the sharp teeth of the enemy.

Quiet is our loving friend. Its balm can soothe us and turn away pain. Sometimes it may be the most important friend we have.

IMPRESSION—SUNRISE, CLAUDE MONET

PERFECTION

"What, after all, is a halo? It's only one more thing to keep clean."
—CHRISTOPHER FRY

WHY DO WE ALL want to be perfect? The ads on TV keep alive this sad desire. The perfect body needs intense and continuous work. Up the step, down the step, on and on. Perfect looks, lots of money, and lots of work. How much do we have to do to become perfect parents, perfect spouses, perfect hosts? The ads tell us how much.

Why are we seduced by this need for perfection? Maybe it's because we think others will love us if we are perfect. (In truth they will most likely be jealous of us.) Perhaps our parents pushed us to strive for perfection. In the deep, black cores of our subconscious minds flash the images of perfection. "Be perfect! Be better than others!"

The only trouble with this approach is . . . everything! We can never be perfect, and if perfection is our goal, then we are condemned to live frustrated lives. "I can't be better, I can't be perfect, so I'm a failure"—an unhappy, foolish failure.

Let's give ourselves a break. Just do the best you can do. That's good enough. That's better than perfect.

FLOWER ON FIRE, CARLA MANZUK

PERFECTION

"I am little concerned with beauty or perfection."

—EMILE ZOLA

DO YOU BELIEVE that you are of a higher order of being than a flea, or a rock, or a deer? If you do, you are a medieval philosopher, one of those people who believed that all beings were arranged in a hierarchy starting with God at the top, down through the angels, through humanity, through the animals, the plants, the minerals, and so on down. The idea of perfection was easy: God is perfect, but a human being can aspire to be only what he is—the best human being possible. This was considered healthy. You couldn't be an angel or God, just a great human being. As this system of thought disappeared, all boundaries dissolved and the neurosis of perfectionism appeared.

A perfectionist carries an enemy within him—the dark angel whispers to him that everything he does must be without flaw, that he at least is not bound by the material and psychological limits of humanity. This dark angel whispers to him in fact that he is God.

Humanity has texture—it can't be perfect. A human being deals with a world filled with other human beings; we can't control all that.

We can be happy, however, being a human being.

Green Dancer, Edgar Degas

PLAY

"The highest form of bliss is living with a certain degree of folly."

—ERASMUS

PUPPIES HAVE THE RIGHT idea: Eat, sleep, and play. Jump and run, stop and go, pounce and pivot and bark. Play and fool around. It's only when they grow up and become dogs that serious responsibilities such as obeying their master interfere with playtime. We humans have many responsibilities and lots of serious work on a daily basis. We don't have much time for play, but we need to make time for it. It is just as important as work. Some brilliant thinkers even believe that play is more important! I am one of them.

So let's get serious about play. Run, jump, pounce, laugh, and dance in the streets and you will feel good. Life will take on a new glow. Work might even become fun. Stress will lessen, and the dreaded anxiety attack can be transformed into a play attack. How, you ask? Here's how.

Approach everything with a smile or a laugh about the absurdity of what life deals us, otherwise we become sick and anxious. Remember that play is an activity, so play golf, play basketball, play at anything, and your body will thank you as much as your mind.

We have plenty to be serious about, so loosen up and laugh. Put life in perspective and this will make you balanced, healthy, and free of anxiety. Let me pounce on that.

LE CIRQUE, GEORGES SEURAT

PLAY

"Play is the key."

—Dr. George Sheehan

SOME PEOPLE CLAIM that creativity begins with play. It seems certainly to be true that play in young children is a generator of the imagination. The child deprived of sense stimuli and toys to play with becomes closed in on himself—a mute little Shakespeare or Fra Angelico or Thomas Jefferson. Fun is a key: What these little people enjoy, they do and do well. Good teachers know this instinctively.

It is a joy to see how quickly young children are drawn to their Legos and dolls and even cardboard boxes and pots and pans. You can almost see their little minds meshing and expanding. It's certainly a great joy of parenthood.

Many adults, however, seem to lose this sense of play, even the play of the mind. No wit, no jokes, no sense of the absurd. As the comedian says, "This is a fine kettle of fish!" A dour, joyless person is one with whom we want nothing to do.

Play, I say with all seriousness, is a necessary activity for any of us who aspire to a happy life or the joys of the imagination.

SUPREMATISM, KASIMIR SEVERINOWICH MALEVICH

RELATIONSHIPS

"I want to be alone."

—GRETA GARBO

WE CAN TRY TO sail our lives alone on the deep, rough sea of life. But this is lonely and dangerous. We can also put ourselves with a flotilla of other ships. This is all a fancy way of saying that we can try to live our lives alone or take the risk of being protected by relationships.

We use the word *relationship* in its oldest sense, where it means a serious contact with other humans—with our children, with our spouses, with our friends, with our co-workers, and with a person we may be living with or are courting. All of these relationships are important to our happiness. How do we handle them?

This little question seems simple, but it is really quite complicated, right on the edge of what it is possible to do with our lives.

But let's try to resolve it simply.

First of all, the relationship itself must be important to us. Our love for our children, spouses, friends, for example, must be deeply meaningful.

Second, we must always put into a relationship as much as we get out of it. Unless this is true, our relationship will dissolve, fall into clay in our hands.

Our relationships protect us from isolation. They bring us experience and love and joy. They are worth our attention because we are the ones who receive all the benefits.

THE HARBOR OF ST. TROPEZ, PAUL SIGNAC

RELATIONSHIPS

"Love doesn't just sit there, like a stone; it has to be made, like bread, remade all the time, made new."

—URSULA K. LE GUIN

WILLIAM BUTLER YEATS ONCE SAID, "To share profound thought and then to touch is the supreme experience of life." This poetic rendering of the truth about relationships is profound.

There are certain constraints in relationships. For it to be good, a relationship must be between two people who respect the necessity for both sharing and solitude. There must be a loving pendulum that always swings between the two needs.

The word *relationship* is overused, but the actuality of listening, loving, giving, receiving, and sharing with another human being is not something we see too often. It must be consciously brought back. To be good and healthy, relationships must be given priority status and be nurtured.

We must share with the other.

We must not try to control the other.

We must give to the other.

We must be willing to receive from the other.

Finally, we must use the kiss of William Blake:

> He who bends to himself a Joy
> Doth the wingèd life destroy
> But he who kisses the Joy as it flies
> Lives in Eternity's sunrise.

BRANCH OF PEONIES, EDOUARD MANET

SECURITY

"I have been poor and I have been rich. Rich is better."

—SOPHIE TUCKER

SECURITY IS NOT JUST a comfort, it is a deep necessity. Spiritual security is important, but let's talk now of the more mundane but equally essential security—the assurance that a person will be able to live. Let's think of rent and food and clothes and medical expenses. When these are in jeopardy, anxiety wrenches apart our every mood and thought so that normal life becomes impossible. When we don't know where the next month's rent is coming from, it's hard to enjoy a movie. The need becomes a negative mantra, setting up in our minds a rhythm and life of its own. "Rent, Rent, Rent." It can become a vicious litany.

Solutions are not easy. The radical answer is to find a way of accepting the idea that somehow it will all work out. This requires an extraordinary control of the movements of our souls—but it is the solution.

The other solutions are practical. How do we get more money? We work harder, maybe longer hours. We make sacrifices. But above all, somehow or other, peace must spread its balm in our minds.

CHICHESTER CANAL, J.M.W. TURNER

SECURITY

"We are moving forward to greater freedom, to greater security for the average man than he has ever known before in the history of America."
—Franklin Delano Roosevelt, *"Fireside Chat"*

ROCKS, TREES, WALLS, and loving arms offer us a deep, warm, mythic comfort. But the fierce winds of imminent risks find little protection in images. The gross fear of the loss of money or shelter or health or even life has a crushing weight of its own. As we push the weight of this fear up the hill, our concentration may be such that we cannot even find time to search for solutions to the problem.

And yet there are always solutions. Christ's resurrection follows his death. Buddha's nirvana follows the deep-grained sufferings. The wisdom of long experience assures us that the pain of insecurity will be followed by the peace and ease of certainty.

But we must learn to deal with the lower parts of the cycle. The certainty that things will change can alleviate the weight of uncertainty. Again, we must search for immediate solutions—a new job, a good doctor, some government assistance—all of these might be open to us.

Finally, the ultimate solution is the belief that there is a loving, higher Being, who will not let us suffer more than we can handle. The support of this loving hand is of inestimable value. Be simple, don't question, allow divine love to care for us.

SPIRIT OF STRUCTURE, EDWARD J. LAVIN, S. J.

SERVICE

"To the memory of the Man, first in war, first in peace,
first in the hearts of his countrymen."
—HENRY "LIGHT-HORSE" HARRY,
Eulogy on the death of George Washington, 1799

I KNOW A HIGH SCHOOL where for the last half of senior year the students are exempted from their classes so that they can devote themselves to some form of service activity. They work in hospitals, schools, or other places that care for others. Each year the faculty can see an enormous change in the students when they return. They seem more mature, more sure of themselves, enriched somehow.

It makes me wonder what changes would happen to all of us if we did such work. What would we be like if our compassion were stirred, if we found others' problems to be more pressing than our own, or if we were to take to our hearts some of the awful consequences of social unbalance? I think we might change a lot and that we would find a fulfillment in our own lives.

I know some people who have great compassion for the poor. They talk a lot about their concern for the disadvantaged, yet they can't stand to be near a poor person—all that smell of hopelessness.

The act of service pulls us out of ourselves, generates in us the power of charity and love, and perhaps most important of all, makes us feel good about ourselves.

PEACOCKS IN THE COUNTRY, PAUL GAUGUIN

SERVICE

"Forward the Light Brigade!
Theirs not to make reply,
Theirs not to reason why,
Theirs but to do and die!

Into the jaws of death,
Into the mouth of hell
Rode the six hundred."

—ALFRED, LORD TENNYSON

IS IT POSSIBLE that our happiness may depend, at least in part, on our service to others? This is a simple question with profound implications. For, like a Japanese rock garden, its answer may be more complex than is immediately apparent.

It is certainly a question that can be faced only in the secret compartments of our own hearts. Are you personally happier when you are helping others? If you are, and I suspect you are, you will have discovered one of the deepest secrets of happiness.

If, on the other hand, you find your heart completely indifferent to the needs of others, I find it utterly useless to try to convince you. I leave you with your indifference and wonder at it.

But if you think that there is some truth in history, I think you will find that literature and biography and simple historical fact will indicate that altruism has produced much more happiness than otherwise.

You are yourself, however, and I join my hand with those who feel the need to help others.

Mammoth Hot Springs, Yellowstone, Thomas Moran

SHARING

"Paradise itself were dim
And joyless, if not shared with him!"

—THOMAS MOORE

AN OLDER GENERATION finds it a little odd and quite charming when we hear the very young say that they are learning about *sharing* in school. We adults never found such a thing in our curriculum. If it takes, the lesson about sharing brings salvation.

An unshared life is like an undrained wound—poisonous and festering and deadly. We have to share our goods—both psychological and material. Think of the person who cannot share his heart. Does not this eminently living organ become hard and lifeless when it is not nourished by the air and light of another person?

We all feel that Scrooge is a pitiful, hateful creature. We are repelled by him and his showers of gold coins. As farfetched as it seems, we all have little Scrooges in our hearts, deaf to the calls of compassion and generosity. God knows, we don't want the ghosts of our lives messing around in our heads. Can't we share a little more and open our hearts?

VIEW OF NIAGARA FALLS FROM THE AMERICAN SIDE, ALBERT BIERSTADT

SHARING

"Behold, I do not give lectures or a little charity. When I give I give myself."
—WALT WHITMAN, *Song of Myself*

MOST OF US HERE in the United States at this time are given a great deal of material and psychological benefits. In our own turmoil we can easily forget this and, even more careless than forgetting, we fail to be grateful for these gifts. Gratitude and sharing are an essential pair—one idea does not exist gracefully without the other.

A system in which we receive and don't give to others is essentially a closed, pernicious process. The receiver becomes like one of those dark, dank cellars where certain types of mushrooms are grown. A bountiful harvest of mushrooms, but what a dull, unhealthy diet.

The light of giving must be let in to bring us joy and appreciation. Can we really appreciate what we are given unless we share it? Unless we do share, we become a suction of expectancy and don't really appreciate or find joy in what we are given. When gifts are expected and claimed as one's right, they tend to become beds of selfishness. Sharing one's gifts is the way to illuminate them and make them precious.

ARIZONA AFTERNOON, BILL FREEMAN

SUCCESS

"Success. Four flights Thursday morning. All against twenty-one mile wind. Started from level with engine power alone. Average speed through air thirty-one miles. Longest fifty-nine seconds. Inform press. Home Christmas."

—ORVILLE AND WILBUR WRIGHT,
Telegram from Kitty Hawk, N.C., DEC. 17, 1903

SUCCESS IS LIKE a half-tamed stallion. It flies with us over the hills and plains of human endeavor. Its power exhilarates us; its streaming mane gives poetry to our most pedestrian efforts. And yet it is a beast—it has a mind of its own and only half-accepts whatever reins we might want to put to its wild ride. We have to be careful. Success is where we want to be, but it can lead to failure much more quickly than the slow plod of a person who hikes the journey of life.

We all want success—why not? We should all have it. But successful success depends on what we want and where we will find it.

Money and fame have their own attractions, but sometimes that dangerous ride is going to hurl us over a cliff in a deadly whirlwind of hooves and reins. It is a philosophical commonplace to notice how dangerous that ride can be.

Suppose that our norm of success is the happiness of our own lives and the lives of those who surround us. That gentle ride might be much more meaningful and attainable. Success is what we judge it to be.

LANDSCAPE IN THE BERNER OBERLAND, FERDINAND HODLER

SUCCESS

"There are two things to aim at in life: first, to get what you want;
and, after that, to enjoy it.
Only the wisest of mankind achieve the second."
—LOGAN PEARSALL SMITH

THERE ARE PEOPLE, very highly principled and intense, who seriously pursue spiritual life. They pray and fast and in principle reject the material values of the culture that surrounds them. They live lives of poverty and chastity and seek God at all times and everywhere. In short they are the Olympians of the spiritual life; they run long interior marathons, they strain all their interior muscles, and achieve a happiness that most of us will never know. They shine from the top of the mountain; they transmit wattages of spiritual energy that leave us breathless.

One of the things they claim to be indifferent to is the whole idea of success. They maintain that substantial reward for effort is not something that is necessary to them. They climb a mountain with only the final goal as their inspiration. But it has occurred to me that this final goal is a most wondrous success.

We less enlightened mortals need some little way stations of success as we ascend our own mountains. In fact it seems to me that the rewards of success are absolutely essential to most of us. Besides, if I have a successful marriage, or raise a successful family, or manage a successful career—what could be wrong with that?

There are some notions of success that are despicable, but they are the obsessions of despicable people. That has nothing to do with us. We can revel in our successes, both spiritual and material.

CAMARGUE, SUNSET, FELIX FRANCOIS ZIEM

WORK

"Ther nis no werkman, what-so-ever he be,
That may bothe werke wel and hastily;
This wol be doon at leyser parfitly."
—GEOFFREY CHAUCER, "The Merchant's Tale," *The Canterbury Tales*

DESPITE ROMANTIC notions to the contrary, I don't think that the workers of this world enjoy their work all that much. The brutalizing scratching at the earth is not really a matrix of happiness and contentedness. The path back to nature is seldom a yellow brick road.

On the other hand, there is a general complaint that much of the work done in the systems of industrial and postindustrial culture is boring, noninvolving, and even brutalizing. The prime analogy of this depressing idea of work used to be the assembly line. Today it might better be portrayed by the image of hundreds of people in a huge room punching information into their computers. What a number.

But what do we do about all this? Work, after all, takes up a lot of our time. First we can find something interesting to do, something that is hard to accomplish; or we can find a way to make it all interesting. There are people who seem to be intensely interested in threading a needle and making something of value with their stitches. We've all met the bus driver who turns an ordinary bus ride into a tour of his city, or the mail carrier who sees his job as a people job, not a paper job. This all has something to do with pride in one's work. No matter what we do with our lives, our work is a reflection of ourselves. It's our choice who we present to the world. Let's do good work today.

THE GLEANERS, JEAN-FRANCOIS MILLET

WORK

"All that matters is value—the ultimate value of what one does."

—JAMES HILTON

THERE USED TO BE, in olden times, a characterization of man as *Homo faber,* man the maker. The Romans felt that this ability to make and construct distinguished man from all other beings. Angels couldn't make anything because they didn't have any hands; the beasts couldn't because they didn't have the intellectual capacity. So making (a kind of work) became one of the distinguishing glories of man—an almost quintessential characteristic of man.

This charming concept is perhaps outdated today, but it does ring some bells. Both men and women can find fulfillment in work to such an extent that when forced to cease working they develop serious problems. Retired men and women may oftentimes find a void within them; they may be haunted by the ghosts of past accomplishments. If other interests don't replace work, then old age of both spirit and body can follow, and death is not far behind.

Isn't that peculiar? Work equals health. Once we realize this, we can more easily tolerate the occasional perception of being caught up in the common grind. Work is glorious; it is like "the air we breathe," a definition of man, an essential ingredient of happiness.

Idle hands and the devil—that is the operative idea.

THE SOWER, VINCENT VAN GOGH

YOUR INNER LIFE

Acceptance
Anger
Closeness to God
Courage
Depression
Detachment
Emotion
Fear
Flexibility
Focus
Happiness
Healing
Intimacy
Joy
Love
Openness
Patience
Peace
Resentment
Self-Deception
Self-Esteem
Self Image
Self-Love
Serenity
Silence

ACCEPTANCE

"Always fall in love with what you're asked to accept. Take what is given and make it over your way. My aim in life has always been to hold my own with whatever's going. Not against; with."

—ROBERT FROST

ACCEPTANCE OF THE THINGS you cannot change is a first step toward peace of mind. Fighting things over which you have no control is a good way to make yourself sick in mind and body. It's better to develop a willingness to change the disturbing situation in your life over which you have some control. The fastest route to discontent is to want something you cannot have and to be blind to all the good you already have. We all see houses and cars we want to own, wish we had more money, and dream about extravagant vacations, but the trick to finding contentment is to enjoy what we have right now. Don't live in your fantasies and wishes, live in the now. Enjoy the beauty of life, not things. There is real joy in accepting friends and family just as they are: I love you, not I love you *but*.

Of course we do not want to be overly passive and accept adversity when we can fight it. First we must accept circumstances as they actually are, and if they are detrimental, we fight to change them. Illness is a good example. We accept the fact that we have a disease and then we become very active in the cure.

There is joy in accepting good fortune and realizing we are worthy of it. As strange as it seems, we must learn to accept gifts and love from others—to respect the generosity of others. And finally, when we accept ourselves, we can live fully. And enjoy life.

MARINE, CLAUDE MONET

ACCEPTANCE

"And that's the way it is."

—Walter Cronkite

Getting up on the horse after you have fallen off is a virtue, I suppose. It isn't always easy. Your own hurt and the rolled-up eyes of the horse make it difficult.

The myth of Sisyphus clearly portrays the pain of constant fruitless effort. He was condemned to push a great rock up a hill, and when he got near the top, it would slip and he would have to start all over again. Bucking one's head against a wall may be a virtue, but surely it is equally virtuous to accept reality and know when to stop.

Acceptance of reality sounds so simple, and yet on a daily basis it can be a real struggle. It seems so logical to accept a situation that we cannot change, and most often logic yields in a clash with feelings. To know when we are faced with an unyielding situation is in itself a wonderful accomplishment. But to accept it! What wisdom! What relief! What virtue!

Once we realize that it is not fear or boredom or laziness that causes us to yield the field with a wave of our hand, then we must accept our adult behavior with relief and joy. Even Superman was killed, but he will return, probably even more super! How right and just!

APPLES AND BISCUITS, PAUL CEZANNE

ANGER

THERE IS A CERTAIN substance that when put into a vacuum will burst into flames. The same thing happens in ourselves when all our personality traits are removed. The vacuum pump sucks out goodness and good judgment, and suddenly we are filled with the flame of anger.

Anger is a force of nature. Like a real fire, if you catch it in time, you can put it out. If you know that a fire is likely to start in a certain place, you can watch for it and put it out. However, once the fire is well started, there is almost nothing that will stop it.

Anger destroys the angry person and all those around him. The angry father can cause fear and terror among his children. The angry wife and mother can manipulate with a force and subtlety that can be felt for years.

Open anger roars through human relations with a destructive force—a fire storm.

The hidden anger that burns and attacks and manipulates can last for years. It destroys the underbrush; it twists and poisons the ground growth.

And so with us. The ferocious exterior flame is uncontrollable except over a long period of work and time. We must isolate our anger and allow it to burn itself out.

Beware of Red, Paul Klee

ANGER

THE FACE OF ANGER is terrifying. When we see that face on the street or in our homes, anger causes us to look away, to draw into ourselves. The destructive blows of anger are painful, clear to those who witness them. More frightening, however, is the interior havoc that this awful emotion can wreak. How hideous those bloody red fires of destruction—the loss of control, the burning of all positive movements of soul. Anger does destroy, at least momentarily, our souls. The angry flow of adrenaline causes damage to our bodies.

And yet anger seems to be natural. It is the control of anger that is required. This is a serious lesson to be learned.

Once anger is upon us in all its ferocity, it seems to be almost impossible to manage. Counting from one to ten is not going to help once our teeth are bared. We have to learn to recognize the general and immediate circumstances that loosen the back draft and then to remove ourselves from those situations.

What about righteous anger? I haven't seen too many examples of it. How can I be right when my reaction is so wrong? I don't believe in expressing anger. It is not worth the emotional energy, and nothing good comes of it.

Montange St. Victoire, Paul Cezanne

CLOSENESS TO GOD

"We human creatures should be at play before the Lord—the higher the play the more pleasing to God."

—SAUL BELLOW

THERE ARE SO MANY people who are unhappy. They cower alone in the midst of enormous dark deserts. They quiver at the edge of black, unfathomable chasms. They tremble, lonely, at the center of the vast battlefields of life.

And yet happiness is there, right at the center of themselves. The deserts can be made green and lush with love. The chasm can be filled with the power of the Spirit. They can be covered with the armor of loving concern. All they have to do is find within themselves the presence of the love and energy and the concern of God.

All we have to do is get close to God.

This is not difficult. God is there waiting for us—within us and all around us.

It is not hard to find God. All we have to do is let him get close to us.

The Buddha says that our minds are like young monkeys imprisoned in a cage for the first time. They yip and yelp; they leap frantically from place to place; they roll their eyes in terror and they find no peace. The image described by the Buddha is so right. If our souls and minds are like those monkeys, we will never get close to God.

The veils that conceal God open only in stillness, in the silent night and day.

It is certain that he is there within us and around us. All we have to do is create the calm space in which we can feel him and recognize him.

I say this to you with all gravity. Happiness is there waiting for you. How easy it is! Just allow the silence that will let you be present to him.

ANGEL LEAVING FAMILY OF TOBIT, REMBRANDT

CLOSENESS TO GOD

"Let go, and Let God."

—ANON.

THINK OF A SOUL, adrift on a dark sea, lost under an infinitely black sky—no sound, no light, no hope. An image of despair. This picture portrays for me the soul without God. God beams to us infinite love, infinite concern, infinite hope. It is this beam of God that can give light to our own sea of despair.

People do live lives without God. Since God is never far from me, I don't know how they handle their moments in the abyss. I consider my belief in God to be a privilege, but I wonder at the absurdity of the times when I allow myself to drift away from him.

Many of us call God to mind only when we are in trouble. This is fine, but so limited. The fulfillment of my being is infinite. Minute finite parts do not satisfy me. Only in the infinite mind and love of God do I find fulfillment and completion. All the rest is finite and limited in comparison.

O God, come within me!
Energize me. Teach me to love!
Open my eyes to infinity!
Make me what I really am!

THE GREEN RIVER, WYOMING, THOMAS MORAN

COURAGE

"Two o'clock in the morning courage: I mean unprepared courage."
—NAPOLEON BONAPARTE

COURAGE IS SOMETIMES dramatic. The soldier who runs into fiery enemy bullets is brave. Equally brave is the firefighter who creeps into a burning room to save a child.

Sometimes courage is less dramatic but no less intense.

The dancer who extends herself beyond her own limits is courageous. So is the person who endures the limits of pain and discouragement to learn how to walk again. Imagine that journey through dark clouds.

The most courageous person I know is a woman who has devoted her life to caring for her severely handicapped son. What a gift of love!

Courage is defined by the idea of risk, the risk of losing something for the benefit of another. We can lose our life, our love, our comfort, our fame, our health, and so forth. But the important thing about courage is the idea that impels us to stand at the edge of the chasm of loss.

After all, the terrorist with grenades strapped to his body is taking a risk. But the perverse ideas that drive him make his risk a madness—not courage.

Courage is a clean, simple virtue. It is powered by love. It declares to the world, "I love this person or thing or idea so much that I will risk for it." The question we must ask is whether we love anything enough to have the courage to defend it. I am sure that we do. We are human. We care. In our small ways and in our big ways we have human greatness. And that is courage.

Napoleon Crossing the Alps, David

COURAGE

"Yes, as my swift days near their goal,
'Tis all that I implore:
In life and death a chainless soul,
With courage to endure."

—EMILY BRONTË, "The Old Stoic"

SOMETIMES COURAGE IS a gentle virtue. We normally think of it in con-
nection with big, heroic events—fires, earthquakes, wars. But the greatest show of
courage is the quiet, insistent facing up to the pressures and hardships of trying to
live our daily lives in a good, moral way.

The alcoholic, or any obsessive person in recovery, must take up the burdens of
his desires each day, one day at a time.

I know a woman who has chronic lower-back pain. The pain is constant and a
torture. Yet she lives her life, a life that is concerned with helping others. Her
courage is immense.

The act of calmly confronting the trials of daily life will never receive any medals,
but it can bring the inestimable rewards of satisfaction and happiness.

Everyone has to live his life, willy-nilly, but the ones who live it well, within good
moral constraints, are the ones whom we admire and hope to emulate. This trip
through life is certainly not as dramatic as walking over a bed of hot coals, but
walking over the shards of our daily lives might require more courage.

Congratulations to those who do it well.

The Rocks of Belle-Ile, Claude Monet

DEPRESSION

"The metaphysical comfort with which, I am suggesting even now, every true tragedy leaves us—that life is at the bottom of things, despite all changes of appearances, indestructibly powerful and pleasurable . . ."
—FRIEDRICH NIETZSCHE, *The Birth of Tragedy*

FOR ANYONE WHO has not experienced such a state, the severely depressed person must be a mystery. His suffering is not an open book. It is almost a complete perversion of what living is all about.

The person suffering from this disease doesn't want to eat; he sleeps either not at all or all the time; the thought of any human contact is excruciating; even more painful is the expectation that he will have to do something. In a larger sense there is an emptiness that one knows will never be filled; there is an actual physical nausea in the throat and esophagus that is constant and debilitating.

This is the extreme. Most of us have experienced some form of depression at times, usually in a milder but still painful form. The feeling of helplessness that lies like a dead mist over the whole life of the depressed person is the most severe block to a cure. But depression can be cured. As frightening as it may seem, one first step is to reorder our interior life. Most times depression will go away by itself, but if the suffering is too intense, see a doctor. There is a light in the darkness—depression can almost always be cured.

LANDSCAPE OF FOREST WITH ROCKS, PAUL CEZANNE

DEPRESSION

"The weariest night, the longest day, sooner or later must perforce come to an end."
—BARONESS EMMUSKA ORCZY

THE THEOLOGICAL WORD for depression is *despair*. *Depression* is a medical word. It denotes a well-defined psychological state with a recognizable list of symptoms. It also presents physical symptoms, another sad list. Several statements summarize the pain: "I would rather die than suffer this pain." "I can't stand to be with other people." "I never want to leave my room or even my bed."

As severe as these desperate feelings are, the spiritual void of despair can be even worse because it attacks us in our deepest spiritual roots. It means a total lack of hope, and hope is the magnet that draws us all to happiness. Perhaps with exaggeration, despair has been called the unforgivable sin. I don't think that any sin is unforgivable, but despair is difficult because it is so hard to forgive ourselves. The flow of God's compassion is infinite, but even it is compromised when we can't allow his soothing grace into our hearts.

Depression and despair will both go away. The gray walls will fall down. In the meantime our love can help those who suffer.

WATERCOLOR, DENISE ABADY

DETACHMENT

"Let it be."

—Paul McCartney

Back in the old days of more muscular spirituality, monks were told that they should be so detached from material things and even from their own will that they should become like an old stick, entirely at the disposal of the superior and indifferent to the vagaries of life.

Not since Twiggy, however, has anyone found any comfort in the notion of being a stick.

But somehow or other, dead stick or not, we have to find a way to deal with the overgrowth of demands, injustices, and burdens that threaten us.

The best machete is the ability to be indifferent to all the vicissitudes of life. Not many of us are capable of this. But we must find a scheme, a method, some spiritual form that allows us to wade through the morass of troubles that threaten to engulf us. A good start would be to be able to recognize what we can't do anything about and to let that go—just let it be—to be able to say, "There is nothing I can do about it." That's a kind of healthy detachment. To be able to *use* the problems of life—that is a holy detachment.

WOMAN IN A WOOD, HEÑRI MANGUIN

DETACHMENT

*"Attachment is the great fabricator of illusions;
reality can be attained only by someone who is detached."*

—SIMONE WEIL

WE LAUGH AT the movie star who makes a trip with forty pieces of luggage. I have a friend who can't seem to make any move without a vast assortment of shopping bags and canvas carryalls. Her arrivals are legendary and in a sense absurd. We are amused by this, but maybe it is a reflection of a more serious journey. The journey of life, the interview journey, the spiritual journey—all of these are images which subconsciously affect our thoughts and emotions.

We should not be encumbered in these journeys, which in some form or other we must all take. An overloaded boat is dangerous; a keel covered with barnacles is exasperating. A clean, neat ship is what we need—no unnecessary burdens.

We must detach ourselves.

Of course each one of us must decide on what is really necessary for his own voyage. A lot of material things could probably be heaved overboard, and some emotional baggage might also be left behind. If we keep it simple for our journey, we might enjoy the scenery more and arrive more surely at our destination.

THE BLUE VASE, PAUL CEZANNE

EMOTION

"She runs the gamut of emotions from A to B."

—DOROTHY PARKER

FOR NEATNESS AND convenience Western philosophers have divided our conscious power into two categories—thought and emotion. This can lead us to valuable insights. But like any division it almost immediately sets us in the arena of value judgments. In this particular comparison, thought has most often emerged as the most valued. Clean, unambiguous, filled with insight, thought charms the intellectual. On the other side of the ring stomps hairy emotion, slightly tinged with the animal, uncontrolled and irrational. Up with thought, the shining, clear champion. Down with the emotions, those terrifying reminders of the real stew of our lives.

And yet thought, most useful in logic and the grand analysis of existence, is only part of our conscious confrontation with life.

In fact, the emotions—fear, anxiety, affection, and so on—all these may be more important to our daily lives. We've got to get a grip on them if we are to have any hope of happiness. A lot of us hide our emotions, and in extreme cases we can even deny their existence. We've got to bring them out of the cave and look at them. We've got to learn to acknowledge them and handle them. Otherwise they become demons and control us.

Imagine a life pervaded by unknown angers and fears. We can tame emotions into powerful stallions that can sweep us over the prairies of life. A gift—the emotions can be a gift or a demon. It is up to us.

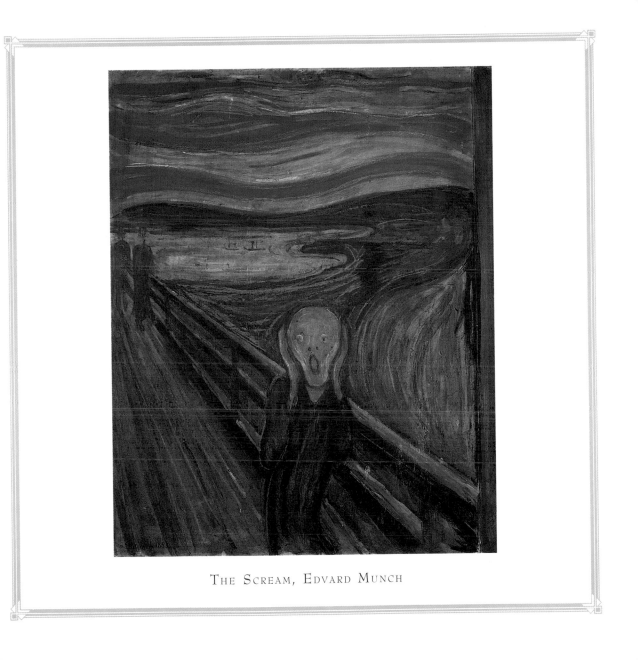

THE SCREAM, EDVARD MUNCH

EMOTION

*"We should take care not to make the intellect our god;
it has, of course, powerful muscles but no personality."*

—ALBERT EINSTEIN

ONCE I HEARD a man say, "This must be true because I like it." This astonishing statement reveals an equally astonishing ignorance of the movements of the mind and soul. Truth is revealed by the light of the intellect—liking is more opaque and is motivated by the emotions.

There is no judgment of quality here. The emotions are as important as the intellect—they just operate in different arenas. An abdication of either the intellect or the emotions is dangerous, sometimes neurotic, and frequently just silly. This is not just an abstraction. There are some sad people who try to live their lives on simple rules of logic. Dull and sad people. There are others who are ruled only by the powerful energies of their emotions. Exciting perhaps but dangerous.

The emotions, those powerful instincts, are essential to our well-being. But we must learn to control them and use them. Raw anger or fear or jealousy can bind us to themselves and rush us into unhappiness. But equally unhappy is the person who has tried to suppress them all.

Be emotional. Feel your feelings, but know that feelings aren't facts.

THE WATERLILIES, CLAUDE MONET

FEAR

"You gain strength, courage and confidence by every experience in which you really stop to look fear in the face. You are able to say to yourself, 'I have lived through this horror. I can take the next thing that comes along.' . . . You must do the thing you think you cannot do."
—ELEANOR ROOSEVELT

WHY DO SOME SITUATIONS make me fearful? Walking along a darkened street with a shadowy person approaching me, I'm afraid. Why? Where is the voice of sweet reason? Under the bed gripped in the bloody claws of the bogeyman.

Is fear only the black clouds of our imagination? Well, sure—fear is about the unknown, something that could happen. When we live in fear, the future threatens us—our life, our body, our security, our well-being, our psyche, our destiny. Are these clouds of the future real? Not usually, but sometimes. Still, we must do the thing we think we cannot do.

Unfortunately we can't usually distinguish between the really imagined and the imagined real. The clouds of fear fog our vision of life. We can become paralyzed in this scary smoke, afraid to move forward. This is the poison of fear our imagination can create. We can't let ourselves become immobilized—turned to stone by the future. Fear is a waste of time. Fear destroys time, ruins lives. Living, growing, changing, and moving forward combat the paralysis of fear. Don't be afraid. There are no bogeymen.

STUDY OF MOUNTAINS, ALEXANDRE CALAME

FEAR

THERE ARE DEMONSTRATIONS of violence that can frighten us and intense expressions of meanness and hatred that can make us shudder. Physical events that are unexpected such as earthquakes or train wrecks can terrify us. These comprise the grand opera of fear. Much less dramatic are the fears that are always with us. They are the ones that debilitate us and render us helpless.

The fear of rejection, the fear for our security, the fear of losing our health.

These and other small fears are the ones that cause the cold and darkness that paralyze us. Are we to find a way out of each one of these particular fears, or should we seek to find a more general solution that renders us immune to the more disastrous consequences of all our fears? A child's fears are dissolved by the loving presence of its mother. Can we find a caring presence who will soften the pain of all our fears? "If God is for me, who can be against?"

I can live a life without fear, but it requires trust, that most elusive of virtues.

CYPRESSES, VINCENT VAN GOGH

FLEXIBILITY

"I bend but I do not break."

—MATTHEW ARNOLD

THERE IS AN OLD analogy, much used but still not trite, that the tree that is able to bend to the winds will last much longer than its stiff-limbed neighbor. Not being able to bend is a danger.

Unfortunately we all tend to get a sort of stiffness of attitude as we get older. The young, seemingly vigorous in their confidence, do in fact shake with insecurity. But one of the common jokes from the comedians in the clubs is the horror of the realization that they are becoming like their fathers and mothers.

Complete flexibility is wimpy, but stiffness is suffocating and demoralizing. We are not condemned to either one or the other. The truth is somewhere in the middle. How sad not to be able to see things anew and with a fresh eye. When one is frozen in attitude, paralysis is the result. An icy-gray sameness will surround us and freeze our lives—no happiness or thrill or ecstasy there—just, maybe, some kind of smug, self-satisfaction. Ugh!

POPLARS ON THE EPTE, CLAUDE MONET

FLEXIBILITY

"A happy and gracious flexibility . . . lucidity of thought . . . freedom from prejudice and freedom from stiffness, openness of mind."

—JEAN DE LAFONTAINE

TO BE ALIVE means to be supple and flexible. Hardening kills, not only arteries but also flowers and even trees. Youth is flexible, but old age, that inexorable decline toward death, brings more and more stiffness. It is a stiffness not only of the knees and the back but of thoughts and attitudes. None of this is necessary.

I know a seventy-year-old man who goes to the gym three times a week and takes ballet class twice a week. His body is like that of a young man, and his attitude toward life is free and joyful. Do you think that all this exercise affects his mental attitude? I do.

How do we keep our minds supple? One way is to be in the uncritical presence of young people. Of course they are sometimes annoying, didactic, and arrogant. But the openness of their attitude is what we want.

The winds of change can be stimulating. But there are also earthquakes in all our lives, seismic tremors that we become much more vulnerable to if we respond with stiffness and resistance. We can swing with the sway or we can tumble down. How satisfied will we then be with our unyielding stance?

COMPOSITION, LIUBOV POPOVA

FOCUS

"The art of being wise is the art of knowing what to overlook."
—WILLIAM JAMES, *The Principles of Psychology*

IN THE EARLY DAYS of movies, filmmakers used to put a piece of cheesecloth over the lens when they shot more mature actors and actresses. This gentle diffusion of focus would mask the ravages of time and hide the harsh realities of the real world.

In the same way many of us do not choose the hard focus when we observe the realities of our lives and worlds. Who wants to stare open-eyed at the miseries that surround us? Give us the soft focus.

Sometimes this lack of focus is healthy. Who wants to be aware of the full sensory assault of a New York subway? The noise, the dirt, the alienation of the passengers—who needs it? A little soft focus is necessary in this experience and others like it.

But there are people who never focus on any of the realities of their lives. This can be dangerous. Never to have a clear picture of ourselves or what is happening around us is too risky. We can't afford the luxury of being an old movie king or queen.

And sometimes reality can surprise us. In sharp focus we can find the beauty of life. We don't have to hide behind cheesecloth.

Bunch of White Peonies, Edouard Manet

FOCUS

"When a man knows he is to be hanged in a fortnight, it concentrates his mind wonderfully."
—SAMUEL JOHNSON, *Boswell's Life of Dr. Johnson*

THERE IS A FORM of meditation in which the participant tries to be aware of everything in his experience. This is practiced in such fine detail that the meditator will note to himself, "Now I am lifting my arm; now my left foot is pressing the ground; now the bird is opening its wings." This kind of awareness is not for all of us.

On the other hand, for many of us lack of awareness is a temptation. How many of the people you know lead almost completely unexamined lives? We don't focus either on ourselves or on the actions and qualities of our lives. Think of making a journey without a map or with a blithe inattention to any of the details of the trip. Would we ever get anywhere, or enjoy ourselves, or escape the dangers of the trip? Just as our attention to planning our vacations will assure us a better time, so planning our lives will do the same. We cannot say that focus is everything, but we can safely say that the unexamined life is no life.

VIEW OF ST. TROPEZ FROM THE CITADEL, FRANCIS PICABIA

HAPPINESS

"Happiness is a warm puppy."

—CHARLES M. SCHULZ

CONTENTMENT IS A BALM, satisfaction is a friendly embrace, but happiness is the warm glow and tingle that arise from the health of both mind and body.

We all want to be happy, yet how many of us can with certainty declare that we are? We all have little happinesses that raise us up out of the mire of our daily struggles. Perhaps we should be content with these small gifts, for the quality of perfect happiness is an uncommon state.

This little caution is a warning to those whose life is a perpetual search for the perfect happiness—a holy grail that requires an immense effort. It is not found in a clean bathroom, although the TV commercials want us to think so. Nor is it found in money or health or friends or lovers or travel or small packages. These may lead to small happinesses, and blessings on them all.

Perfect happiness is a well-regulated hierarchy of spirit, mind, and body. The order is important, and anything that disturbs that order ruffles the surface of the lake of happiness. Unregulated desire, as the Buddha knew so well, is a heavy stone dropped into the lake; equally disturbing is the tendency to forget about the spirit and to concentrate exclusively on the mind or the body. Perfect happiness is not to be found in the leaps of aerobic movement nor in the dense concentration of scholarly research.

Yet we must not despair. Perfect happiness is our birthright—it is only that we must work at it.

Le Chahut, Georges Seurat

HEALING

THE SOUL HEALS and science cures. This new distinction between healing and curing is not so easy to understand, but it is easy enough to experience. The intricate numbers and endless repetitions of science create giant scalpels and almost magical potions to destroy the dark diseases within us. A friend of mine has one hundred and fifty stitches in his abdomen to remind him of the skill of the surgeon who removed the cancer there. He receives a shot every month to prevent any recurrence. Miraculous! But there are other things that can only be healed by the warm, powerful energies of his soul. "Intimation of mortality," examinations of life, powerful feelings of loss—all these were made well by the light generated in his soul.

But—and this is the new question—can the light and energy of the soul help in the cure, not just in the healing? Many medical people think it can. A loving hand and a balance of the soul can affect the cells of the body. In many places meditation has become an acceptable part of the cure.

Dopo la pioggia. La Veranda bagnata, Aleksandr Gherasimov

HEALING

"Healing is a matter of time, but it is sometimes also a matter of opportunity."
—HIPPOCRATES

THE IMMUNE SYSTEM is the new magician. It makes all these complicated passes and sends its powers to kill and drive out our enemies. Its dark side is terrifying, but it does so much for most of us. Can this system be set in motion or be strengthened by means other than physical? In other words, do mental and spiritual healing work?

Meditation is said to be healing. If this is true, this wonderful practice, which is itself both spiritual and mental, becomes a wonderful resource for healing. There are no analytical reasons to compel us to believe in the power of meditation, but there is a lot of anecdotal evidence. Doctors and nurses and sick people believe that they are healed by meditation. Immune systems are affected by mental and spiritual powers.

A person relaxes, empties his mind, and images the healing of the destructive forces within himself. This is a beautiful thought, and I urge it upon you. Peacefulness, positive image-making, faith, quietude—all are states of the mind and of the soul. They all bring us the gentle balm of healing. I am not attempting to prove anything. I only want you to try what others have found to be a salvation. The doses of the medical profession are potent, but they may not be the only answer. One hopes not.

Mont St. Victoire, 1885–1887, Paul Cezanne

INTIMACY

For such,
Being made beautiful overmuch
Consider beauty a sufficient end,
Lose natural kindness and maybe
The heart-revealing intimacy
That chooses right, and never find a friend.

WILLIAM BUTLER YEATS

To WHAT CAN I compare a life without intimacy? Is it old before its time, is it dried up, is it sad? It is all of these things and more. The closeness of intimacy is a risk. It breaks down walls and fills in moats and dissolves the psychic space with which we surround ourselves. The risk of rejection is real, as is the fear of dependence.

Wouldn't it be better not to risk it? This is the same as asking whether it wouldn't be better not to experience one of the most exciting and sweetest joys a human being can experience.

The physical intimacy of a simple touch or the astonishing excitement of the act of love give the body the dimension and sensory experience that complete it. Intimacy of mind and spirit; just as important, give us the chance to nurture and communicate at an equally profound level.

It would be a great loss to miss all this. We could spend a lot to purchase the field in which this treasure is hidden.

THE PARLIAMENT IN LONDON, STORMY SKY, CLAUDE MONET

JOY

". . . The very bird,
grown taller as he sings, steels
his form straight up. Though he is captive,
his mighty singing
says, satisfaction is a lowly
thing, how pure a thing is joy."

—MARIANNE MOORE

WHEN I LOOK INTO the crevices of the world, dark movements assault my eyes. Evil makes me sad. On the contrary, the great movements of the universe expand my heart, and fill me with joy.

What I mean is this: when I am connected to great persons (God) and great ideas (truth, service, justice) and great emotions (love, energy), these things carry me to the outside limits of myself where the waves of joy crash over my life.

But there are great sorrows, too. The four horsemen swoop down from the clouds —disease, war, famine, death—and the pain shoots out from beneath the horses' hooves to leave us desolate and sad from the seeming injustice.

But even these monumental sadnesses are swept into insignificance by the great wind of the spirit. When open ourselves to the vast pulse of the love of God—the spirit of the universe—we find ourselves filled with uncontrollable joy.

Little sorrows are changed into joys.
Great sorrows are swept up into the vast love of
the Universe.
Joy is the love of God.

UNTITLED, WASSILY KANDINSKY

JOY

"The most useless day of all is that in which we have not laughed."
—SÉBASTIEN ROCH NICOLAS CHAMFORT

JOY IS THE EXUBERANT external face of happiness. It rushes up from the quiet flows and waves of contentment and satisfaction. Whereas happiness is a condition of longer duration, caused by a proper fit of our lives into the puzzles of reality, joy is more like a single event, an expression of something that invades our lives in a single, quick, unexpected flash.

Heard under the proper circumstances, in a single brilliant performance, a symphony of Beethoven can take our hearts right out of us.

Sometimes a single act of love can transport us into the blessed realms of joy.

Recently I attended an Easter-egg-hunt party, and the picture of the innocent children, their colors painted on the green of a perfect lawn, sent me out of myself into a sweet lightening of joy. It was unexpected and heartbreakingly beautiful.

I have most often thought of joy as a gift. It comes to a heart open and for a brief moment unsullied by the self. There is so much beauty in the world just waiting for us.

LE MOULIN DE LA GALETTE, PIERRE-AUGUSTE RENOIR

LOVE

"All mankind loves a lover."

—RALPH WALDO EMERSON

HERE IS THE IMAGE: the whole universe energized by love. The force of love causing the great swings of the galaxies. The passion of love lighting the intense energy of the stars. The fantastic power of growth and reproduction of all of the life forces of the worlds. All of these forces are love. That's the image. The beauty of the concept can break your heart.

The idea of this energy, the force of love, is not so farfetched to the Christian believer. Follow the idea: (1) God the Father relates to God the Son by love; (2) this love is personified into the Holy Spirit; (3) the Spirit (love) is the divine, all-pervasive energy of the creation. And so, as in the Trinity made poetic, it represents the force of gravity in love, the power of life in love, the intensity of light in love.

Does this lead us to the charming conclusion that the attraction of atoms to one another means that they are "in love"? Logic compels the idea, and poetry embellishes it.

We who can freely give love or refuse it make an enormous choice—to become part of the deepest energies of creation or to be alienated from them. Love does make the world go round. Are you part of the great circle, or have you closed yourself off from it?

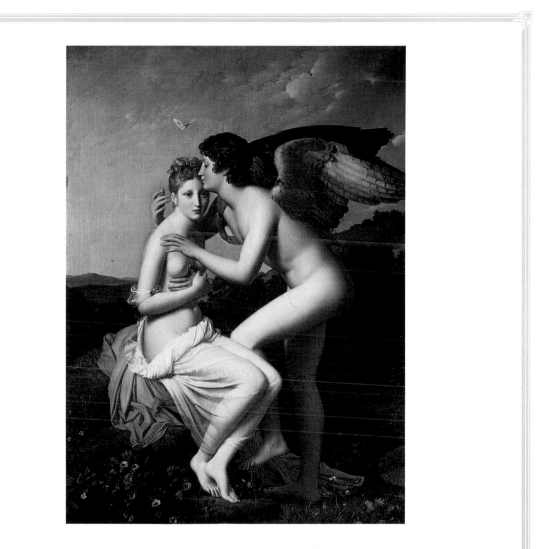

PSYCHE AND AMOR, FRANCOIS GERARD

LOVE

"And love can come to everyone,
The best things in life are free."
—BUDDY DESYLVA, 1927 song, "Good News"

LOVE IS A "MANY-SPLENDORED thing." It is also the deepest and most exalted of human feelings. The wings of love carry us up out of ourselves. They take us to wondrous places unimagined; they change us into beings without bounds.

The poetry of love is glorious and sweet. Its reality can be more prosaic. Love is not elitist. Anyone is capable of love. Love is built on a structure of giving, the strength of which we may not be willing to give in to. It is a lasting commitment, an obligation that we may feel is beyond us.

There have been great songs of praise about love. Even the normally prosaic Saint Paul declares in 1 Corinthians; 13:4–7 that "Love is patient, love is kind. It does not envy, it does not boast, it is not proud. It is not rude, it is not self-seeking, it is not easily angered, it keeps no records of wrongs. Love does not delight in evil but rejoices with the truth. It always protects, always trusts, always hopes, always perseveres." How about that for a list of qualities? They are the strong feathers of the wings of love. We fly with them into realms of ecstasy. We fly as high as a human being can go. A life without love is only half a life. We can survive without it, but what a loss to be half happy or half fulfilled. How sad when we could be filled with the glory of love!

BOUQUET OF FLOWERS, ODILON REDON

OPENNESS

"People are lonely because they build walls instead of bridges."
—Joseph Fort Newton

THERE ARE PEOPLE you meet who are like a swamp—closed, dark, dank. Not very inviting. There are others who are like a mountain—open, clean, filled with light. I'm not particularly anxious to meet the swamp person, but the openness of the mountain person fills me with joy. We human beings are born to communicate, to be open.

The closed person is sad, filled with fear, closed to new experiences. The open person is just the opposite—happy, filled with courage.

We must all try to be open. Without that characteristic we cannot change, we cannot learn, we cannot communicate on any high level.

All of life brings risks with it. Falling in love is risky. Shall we close down and never fall in love? What a dreary sadness. But how grand it is to be open—open to love, open to learning, open even to hurt.

The great athlete opens himself to great risks and achieves great results. Michael Jordan risks a lot in a jump toward the basket, but the great shot makes it worth it!

Picasso opened himself to the risk of ridicule and he let in beauty.

Christ opened himself to the risk of love and he conquered death.

Open up—let the risk and the sunshine in.

MONTEREY COAST, THOMAS MORAN

PATIENCE

"The strongest of all warriors are these two—Time and Patience."
—LEO NIKOLAEVICH TOLSTOI

PATIENCE IS NEITHER weariness nor dreary surrender. It is a positive virtue, the capacity to wait for opportunity, a necessary weapon in our armament of life.

There are many images that portray patience: The lioness waiting in the high grass for her prey to pass by, making no movement for hours except for gentle twitches of her tail. The old monk waiting for God; the ancient eyes filled with wisdom, his mind and body filled with tranquillity. Another image is the picture of the slow growth of the solid oak tree. Imperceptibly, little by little, the acorn becomes a tree. Slowly—that's how it becomes so strong.

We live in a time when speed seems to be essential. Fast trains, fast cars, fast walking, fast-food restaurants. Even our perception of growth is speeded up with the use of the stop-frame camera.

There is nothing wrong with speed in itself, but a question is forced upon us. Does speed necessarily require us to be unreflective? If so, then we are rushing into lives that are not reflected upon, not examined. This is dangerous. Perhaps we do have to make room for patience in our lives—a little room to breathe. Patience. Patience.

WATERLILIES—SETTING SUN, CLAUDE MONET

PEACE

THERE IS A POEM by Robert Browning in which he describes a Spanish monk standing at a window looking out at another monk working in the garden. The first monk says about the other, "Grrr—there goes my heart's abhorrence." And so this figure, so peaceful in appearance, in this setting so tranquil, is really filled with a whirlwind of hatred.

Peace is of course a great gift, something we instinctively search out. We know that it will give us health of mind and body. Yet we so misunderstand it that we look for it in all the wrong places. Is it found in a cloistered monastery? Not necessarily. Is it found on a quiet beach or in a deserted woods? Not necessarily. There are people who think it can be found in drugs. No peace in drugs, only pain. There might be oblivion for a while, but then the dragon of addiction comes to shatter our castle of clay.

It is in our own heart that peace is found. The heart that has found its own inner tranquillity can find peace anywhere, anytime.

"Be still, my beating heart" and I put you on the subway and you find peace. I could put you on the treadmill of anxiety, and if you reach deep enough, there is peace.

If you meditate, your heart will surely be still. And peace is yours.

Rest, Belimbao

PEACE

THE MOST COMMON use of the word *peace* is as the opposite of *war*. This is understandable but unfortunate. Peace is not just the opposite of violence or turmoil but has a whole register of meanings all its own. The peace of a quiet landscape nurtures us. A calm moment to ourselves renews our energies. Interior peace energizes us; exterior peace gives us direction. A gentle sun, a calm ocean, the loving smile of a friend—all of these give us peace. We are sustained in a sweet aerie of calm.

The opposite of peace is war, but so are agitation, anxiety, and violence. Our culture is on the verge of teaching us that violence is fine as long as the "good guy" wins in the end. So violence of thought and word and action creeps up on us, and we have to watch out that it doesn't explode into our relationships and social activities. A mean word spoken to our children is as real a sword as that of Attila.

Finally, with great simplicity, we can say that peace is better than war.

Peace to us all.

BRIDGE AT ARGENTEUIL, CLAUDE MONET

RESENTMENT

"Nothing on earth consumes a man more quickly than the passion of resentment."
—FRIEDRICH NIETZSCHE

RESENTMENT IS A great waste of time. The person you resent has no idea that you are totally disturbed by their existence and as you ruin your day with negative thoughts and dreams of revenge, the person you resent is probably having a perfectly good day. What a terrible waste resentment is.

How wonderful it would be if the people with whom we get even are the people who do us good. Without fail we can kill our own resentment if we pray for the person we resent. It is impossible to feel upset while you invoke good for another human being. We have all experienced this feeling. There was a young woman who had an overwhelming resentment toward her mother-in-law because she thought that this woman had caused her divorce. She was consumed with bad thinking and suffered excruciating headaches and insomnia. Willing to try anything to stop this self-destruction, she prayed for her mother-in-law. Almost miraculously the resentment disappeared. Her life with her small child resumed normalcy, and she discovered that resentment never again appeared in her life. The cure works. So if resentment poisons your life, pray for the person.

BALLON ROUGE, PAUL KLEE

RESENTMENT

"Let us not look back in anger or forward in fear, but around in awareness."
—JAMES THURBER

THERE ARE POISONS that are particularly virulent to the human condition. One of these is resentment. This particular virus brings fever, chills, and weakness. For as with a fever, we become oversensitive, and the chills of resentment paralyze our thoughts and feelings and cause the death of happiness in our lives.

What a waste of time to focus so completely on real or imagined wrongs! Sometimes resentment leaves no time or room for anything else—a whole mind and heart that is filled with dark clouds of anger. The waste of energy and concentration is atrocious. In more serious cases of resentment, a whole life can be consumed by thoughts of injuries or slights or insults. What a waste!

Do we want to give another person such power over us? In many instances the resentment we bear is much more destructive than the act that seemed to cause it. And thus we are hurting ourselves. Think about that for a moment: Most of the hurt caused by resentment comes from ourselves.

This minihatred is a killer of joy and happiness. Forgiveness of the "enemy" could be the solution. Certainly self-pity is not—it can never help anything.

RAINBOW OVER NIAGARA FALLS, THOMAS MORAN

SELF-DECEPTION

*"Nothing is easier than self-deceit. For what each man wishes,
that he also believes to be true."*

—DEMOSTHENES

THE LIGHT THAT illumines the way to health and spiritual maturity is *truth*. Deception, especially self-deception, blocks the heart and the mind; most seriously it perverts the Spirit. If you lie to yourself, you suffer. You suffer because you lose your identity. When you lie to yourself, that's pitiful.

There are people who splash paint on their clothing so that they will be known as artists, but there's no truth, no art, in that. Pick up the brush, have the courage to paint the picture, and create the art. Face the truth.

The rap dance of the person who manipulates a personal relationship blocks true emotion and infects the atmosphere of love. When you manipulate, you choke human relationships. It's a lonely life, just you and your lies.

Lies are like the distorting mirrors in a fun house: no reality—too tall, too thin, too fat. Is the distortion frightening? Real reality is okay. Hiding from it will destroy you.

Self-deception allows no reach to reality, no blossoming of love, no stretch of the Spirit.

MONT ST. VICTOIRE ABOVE THE ROAD OF THOLONET, PAUL CEZANNE

SELF-DECEPTION

"Men willingly believe what they wish."

—Julius Caesar

It seems odd that we can fool ourselves so easily about ourselves. After all, the subject matter is us, a thing we should know quite clearly. There is no distance between the knower and what is to be known—it should be easy to know ourselves. And yet what clouds of deception warp and misfocus our knowledge about ourselves! What is going on?

For one thing pride and vanity are going on. A whole parade of wishful thinking deceives me. "More attractive, more intelligent, more talented." The drums bang and the bugles blare, and there march I, the hero of my own mind.

Second, truth is misted over by desire. I see myself not as I am but as I would like to be. I feel that I am the very paragon of love, and yet my selfishness leaves others gasping. I know that desire is not truth, and yet my mind can contort reality until it seems so.

Self-deception is dangerous because reality has a way of revealing itself in large or small flashes. These real moments of truth can cast us down into the depths of shame and fear. The undeceiving of the deceiver is hard, but we can learn a lesson from it—that we, as we really are, are good enough; there is no need for self-deception.

CASTLE AND SUN, PAUL KLEE

SELF-ESTEEM

"Just trust yourself, then you will know how to live."
—JOHANN WOLFGANG VON GOETHE

THE PERSON WHO does not love himself is out of balance—there is a missing cog in his wheels, a blot on the blueprint of his life. Perhaps we should use the word *self-esteem* rather than *self-love*. The latter calls up images of selfishness and excessive involvement with the self, so *self-esteem* may be the more proper term. I can use it easily without hearing my mind boiling with contradiction and qualification. And used properly, self-esteem can generate positive forces in our lives.

Humility is also a force. It keeps us honest, but it can also be dangerous. Saint Thomas Aquinas defines *humility* as "the truth." Truth keeps us honest, but when we use false humility, it can become an excuse for inaction or laziness or neurosis. "I could never do that. I'm not capable of that." These kinds of statements could be true or they could be excuses.

Self-esteem is the joyful antidote for this kind of destructive virus. "Of course I can do it, or at least I will try my hardest." This affirmation is charged with positive vibrations. I salute you, I commend your attitude. I will help you in whatever way I can!

BALLET REHEARSAL ON STAGE, EDGAR DEGAS

SELF-IMAGE

"I myself am more divine than any I see."

—Margaret Fuller

NO MATTER WHAT one's beliefs, the intellectual theology about the Trinity is very interesting. God the father is the creator; the Son or Logos is the image of all created things; and the Holy Spirit is the creative force that shapes outside reality.

This of course reads like the quiet adventure we all go through as we create ourselves. We are the creator, our emotions are the creative energy, and our memories and imaginations provide the image of ourselves that we are working for. Self-image is difficult, there is no doubt about it. But a strong, clear gaze into ourselves is not only necessary, it can bring us contentment. How pleasing to be what one is and not to have to throw up false images on the screens of our minds and emotions. Truth can hurt, but what a relief!

Of course we can lose the desire to work on ourselves, and our emotions can run riot, but the self-image is the most unstable and tricky element of the whole process. We can fool ourselves too high or too low, but if we are plain and open, sooner or later we can come to the proper image—truthful, not overstretched, and not underestimated. Our true selves projected and made real.

SENECIO, PAUL KLEE

SELF-LOVE

"To love oneself is the beginning of a lifelong romance."

—OSCAR WILDE

THERE IS A NEW axiom of sidewalk psychology. It says with a reverse twist that we will never be able to love each other unless we love ourselves first. This is quite true if we take it in a tough, analytic sense. If we consider ourselves to be worthless or not worthy of consideration, how can we have the power to absorb the great forces of another love?

The axiom about love of self has a dark side. It is used by some people as an excuse to be concerned only about themselves. This particular poison is deadly, and like an odorless gas it can destroy without warning.

We can be gentle hypocrites or, to put it simply, we can fool ourselves into thinking that we are following some important accepted wisdom when in fact all we are doing is being selfish. The "I" is important, but the "we" may be our salvation.

Think it through; be wise; be honest. I can love myself to my destruction or to my salvation.

THE REAPER, WINSLOW HOMER

SERENITY

"Mirth is like a flash of lightning, that breaks through a gloom of clouds, and glitters for a moment; cheerfulness keeps up a kind of daylight in the mind, and fills it with a steady and perpetual serenity."

—JOSEPH ADDISON

THE EYE OF A HURRICANE must be an interesting place. All that calm surrounded by the most violent force and noise and movement. In most instances turmoil is our enemy. It blows through our souls and tenses our bodies. Adrenaline overload becomes our storm shelter. Noise in the street invades and tenses our sleep. We are victims of clamor. Our minds and imaginations are affected with their own clamor. The high tension of the TV and the powerful threats of insecurity tear up the tranquillity of our souls.

And where do we find serenity? Mountains and seashores appear to us like psychic antibiotics. Yet this kind of escape is rarely practicable, and besides, some kinds of agitation are carried with us in our hearts. Our souls and minds are also filled with static, and we must fine-tune our own serenity of soul.

This serenity of soul is a thing we must covet. Its peace can spread out from our interior to all the parts of our bodies—a balm of quiet. Meditation, that deliberate creation of quiet, can help in all of this. Stripped of all its mystification, it may be the salvation of us all.

Landscape, Paul Gauguin

SERENITY

"I have laid aside business, and gone a-fishing."
—IZAAK WALTON, *The Compleat Angler*

SOMETIMES WE MEET people who have an aura of peace, calm, and compassion—an aura of serenity. One can be greatly moved by this encounter. It is a kind of presence, one that is at the same time so compelling and so attractive that it affords a view of the vast horizons that are open to human nature—an infinite light, a cosmic kindness, an openness that never closes.

Sometimes we come across these saints in a religious context—an old nun, a wise rabbi. Sometimes this encounter takes place in a Twelve Step setting, such as Alcoholics Anonymous, or even sometimes in a more worldly atmosphere. Wherever it happens, it can leave us with the nagging wonder whether or not we can share in that powerful energy.

We can note that most of the time these wonderful people are older—more mature in years as well as in attitude. This means that these qualities take hold over a period of time. There is no storming of castles, just the slow erosion of selfishness and pride and self-absorption. Besides, this energy is generated from a lifetime of love for others. Can we do this? Surely we can.

PERIODS OF LIFE, CASPAR DAVID FRIEDRICH

SILENCE

"Silence is the perfectest herald of joy: I were but little happy, if I could say how much."
—William Shakespeare, *Much Ado About Nothing*

We CARRY OUR own silence with us. Unfortunately we can also bring with us, wherever we go, a din of crushing and deafening noise. It's not clear why, but there are people who need the companionship of noise. It must make them feel less lonely. But it is pathetic—a noisy parade wherever they go. Who needs it?

There are men and women who are gifted with quiet. It flows out of them almost like a force of nature. One imagines the depths of Spirit and personality out of which it emanates. Their presence comforts us and soothes us with their "sounds of silence."

How necessary is silence to us? I think it depends on personality—some of us need more silence than others. But I don't know of any healthy person who can live in constant noise. There are voices within us that must be heard only in silence. There are still little imitations of reality—little seeds of happiness and germs of future problems that we miss only at great risk.

An aura of silence is very appealing. God knows we all need that.

ROUEN CATHEDRAL IN THE MORNING, CLAUDE MONET

SILENCE

"The deepest feeling always shows itself in silence."
—MARIANNE MOORE

STATIC, SIRENS, SHOUTING, emotional storms—all these kind of noises zap our energy, frighten us, or distance our vision. We all yearn for peace and especially for that part of it that is silence.

We all think that silence would be lovely. Many of us think that we would like to make a retreat, to walk in quiet cloisters and sit alone in a monastery garden. This is glorious, but after a brief trial these people, imaginary monks, begin to feel the silence as oppressive. Silence must be filled with things of even deeper silence, such as prayer or reflection in the presence of God.

For those of us who don't have the privilege of living in a quiet place, there is an alternative. We must learn to carry our own silence with us—different-sized envelopes of quiet that will protect us from the pollution of both interior and exterior noise.

How do we learn to do this? By sitting in short periods of deliberately planned silence. This kind of quiet can become a habit that can be summoned to our attention and aura. We can ride a subway train with our own personal islands of serenity and silence. A triumph of the spirit!

Internal noises can also be silenced—by acceptance and resignation and prayer. The saint does this with ease. We minisaints can learn it with practice.

Orange Trees and Gate, Winslow Homer

PERMISSIONS AND ACKNOWLEDGEMENTS

Grateful acknowledgement is made to Art Resource and Scala/Art Resource, National Museum of American Art, Smithsonian Institution/Art Resource, Giraudon/Art Resource, Eric Lessing/Art Resource, Alinare/Art Resource, Tate Gallery, London/Art Resource, Jian Chen/Art Resource, Kavaler/Art Resource, for permission to use the works of art printed herein.

Grateful acknowledgement is made to Artists' Rights Society for permission to use the painting UNTITLED by Wassily Kandinsky, © 1993 ARS, NY/ADAGP, Paris.

Grateful acknowledgement is made to artists Bill Freeman, Carla Manzuk, and Susanne Nyberg for permission to print their paintings in this book.

Grateful acknowledgement is made to Warner/Chappell Music, Inc. for permission to reprint lyrics from song GOOD NEWS (Lew Brown, Ray Henderson, B.G. DeSylva) © 1927 (renewed) RAY HENDERSON MUSIC, CHAPPELL & CO. & STEPHEN BALLENTINE MUSIC PUBLISHING CO. All rights for the World, ex. U.S. and Canada, administerd by CHAPPELL & CO. All rights for the U.S. administered by CHAPPELL & CO., RAY HENDERSON MUSIC, and STEPHEN BALLENTINE MUSIC PUBLISHING CO. All rights reserved.